THE WORKS OF WILLIAM H. BEVERIDGE

Volume 7

A BEVERIDGE READER

A BEVERIDGE READER

Edited by
KAREL WILLIAMS & JOHN WILLIAMS

Routledge
Taylor & Francis Group

LONDON AND NEW YORK

First published in 1987

This edition first published in 2015
by Routledge
2 Park Square, Milton Park, Abingdon, Oxon, OX14 4RN

and by Routledge
711 Third Avenue, New York, NY 10017

Routledge is an imprint of the Taylor & Francis Group, an informa business

British Library Cataloguing in Publication Data
A catalogue record for this book is available from the British Library

ISBN: 978-1-138-82643-4 (Set)
eISBN: 978-1-315-73730-0 (Set)
ISBN: 978-1-138-82999-2 (Volume 7)
eISBN: 978-1-315-73748-5 (Volume 7)

Publisher's Note
The publisher has gone to great lengths to ensure the quality of this reprint but points out that some imperfections in the original copies may be apparent.

Disclaimer
The publisher has made every effort to trace copyright holders and would welcome correspondence from those they have been unable to trace.

A
Beveridge Reader

KAREL WILLIAMS
JOHN WILLIAMS

London
ALLEN & UNWIN
Boston   Sydney   Wellington

Allen & Unwin, the academic imprint of
Unwin Hyman Ltd
PO Box 18, Park Lane, Hemel Hempstead, Herts HP2 4TE, UK
40 Museum Street, London WC1A 1LU, UK
37/39 Queen Elizabeth Street, London SE1 2QB, UK

Allen & Unwin Inc.,
8 Winchester Place, Winchester, Mass. 01890, USA

Allen & Unwin (Australia) Ltd
8 Napier Street, North Sydney, NSW 2060, Australia

Allen & Unwin (New Zealand) Ltd in association with
the Port Nicholson Press Ltd,
60 Cambridge Terrace, Wellington, New Zealand

First published in 1987

British Library Cataloguing in Publication Data

Beveridge, William Henry Beveridge, *Baron*
  A Beveridge reader.
1. Economics – Great Britain – History
– 19th century   2. Economics – Great
Britain – History – 20th century
I. Title   II. Williams, Karel
III. Williams, L.J.
330.1   HB103.A2
ISBN 0–04–361070–6

Library of Congress Cataloging-in-Publication Data

Beveridge, William Henry Beveridge, Baron, 1897–1963.
  A Beveridge reader.
Bibiliography: p.
Includes index.
1. Economics – Great Britain – History.   2. Beveridge,
William Henry Beveridge, Baron, 1879–1963.   3. Great
Britain – Economic policy.   I. Williams, Karel.
II. Williams, John (L. John)   III. Title.
HB103.A2B48 1987   338.941   87–11819
ISBN 0–04–361070–6 (alk. paper)
ISBN 0–04–361071–4 (pbk. : alk. paper)

Typeset in 10 on 12 point Sabon by Phoenix Photosetting, Chatham
and printed in Great Britain by Billing and Son, Worcester

Contents

Acknowledgements

We are grateful to the following organizations who have kindly given permission for the reproduction of copyright material: *The Daily Mail*, Longman, National Deposit Friendly Society. Crown copyright material is reproduced by permission of the Controller of Her Majesty's Stationery Office.

A
Beveridge Reader

General Introduction:
Beveridge's Collectivism

Beveridge's first book was published in 1909 and his last appeared in 1960. In the years between Beveridge wrote at least twenty books and official reports as well as several pamphlets and a large number of short journalistic pieces. Three of his books are still referred to and read by historians and social administrators. The three 'classic' texts are the book *Unemployment: a problem of industry* (1909) and two reports of the 1940s – the official report on *Social Insurance and the Allied Services (SIAS)* (1942) and the unofficial report on *Full Employment in a Free Society* (1944). Beveridge's oeuvre also includes four volumes of collected journalism (1935, 1943, 1944 and 1945) and several forgotten texts on problems of economic and social policy – *British Food Control* (1928), *Tariffs* (1932), *Voluntary Action* (1948) and *Evidence for Voluntary Action* (1948). As though this were not enough, we must remember that Beveridge also published on a variety of themes which have little or nothing to do with modern economic and social policy. His 'other books' include a history of wages and prices in England over seven hundred years (1939), a biography of his parents (1947) and a history of the London School of Economics (1960).

This reader reprints selected extracts of this large body of published material. The size of the oeuvre is such that what is presented inevitably and obviously offers a partial reading. And, in this case, the first task is to explain the principles of construction which have been applied in the choice of extracts. Without such an explanation, the editors would inevitably impose their undisclosed preconstructions on those who use the reader. The task of explanation is all the more important because many who use this reader will not be able to check the original texts and set the extracts into context. All of Beveridge's books are out of print and many of them have been out of print for so long that they are only available in larger research libraries.

Our reader is designed to pose and answer one rather abstract question: what was the nature of Beveridge's collectivism? This issue is directly taken up in the first chapter, on 'the economic and social philosophy of a free society'. This first chapter reproduces extracts from various texts of the 1930s and 1940s written when Beveridge was developing and articulating the philosophy of state action which we call 'liberal collectivism'. It may seem eccentric to put the latter philosophy in the foreground in this way. After all, Beveridge wrote practical problem-centred books on economic and social objects and instruments like unemployment, full employment, poverty, social insurance and friendly societies. None of this sounds very philosophical. But our central argument is that Beveridge's choice of discursive object and his preference among policy instruments were consistently determined by a liberal political philosophy which develops and becomes more explicit in the forty years after 1909. This theme is taken up and developed in the four later chapters of this reader. Chapters 3 and 4 examine the development of Beveridge's ideas about social insurance and unemployment over forty years; in these areas it is a question mainly of tracing the influence of his developing liberalism on interim problems and solutions. The other chapters are concerned with the mature Beveridge and his final position. Chapter 2 demonstrates that liberal collectivism determined almost every detail in his 1942 design for a comprehensive social insurance scheme, while Chapter 5 shows that Beveridge's views about private welfare developed in the same philosophical medium.

In a famous aphorism, Dicey claimed that 'legislative opinion is itself more often the result of facts than of philosophical speculation'. This claim is wrong because it rests on a false antithesis between the factual and the philosophical. Beveridge's work shows how facts (and policy instruments) are constructed in and through political philosophy. The short editorial introductions to each chapter of readings are designed to establish this point and to provide basic background information on particular issues. The introductions to the chapters do not criticize the originality or general intellectual quality of Beveridge's texts. If we applied this criterion, Beveridge would not do well. Keynes, for example, aspired to and, with the *General Theory* in 1936, did achieve greater originality in the field of economics where all of Beveridge's writings were conventional, secondary and derivative. But this comparison misses the point, which is that Beveridge's speciality was the packaging of progressive reformist ideas that others originated; in economics Beveridge's legacy was the classic British popular exposition of Keynesianism in the 1944 text *Full Employment*. In this and other texts, Beveridge had the political insight to see that new technical ideas could be used as a means to the realization and development of old philosophical principles. The conclusion to this reader is therefore properly focused on the philosophy of liberal collectivism itself.

Beveridge has so far been treated as a problem in, and for, the history of ideas. But that question is of interest mainly because it raises issues about the modernization of economic and social policy and more specifically about the design of the post-1945 policy settlement which created a welfare state based on comprehensive social insurance and Keynesian full employment. Beveridge's role as architect of this settlement was partly sustained through the writing of key texts. We would not wish to equate this role simply with the writing of texts. His official career in social administration as a civil servant after 1908 and again after 1934 allowed him to influence events more directly. Equally, we would not wish to claim that governments, like the Liberal government before 1914 or the Labour government after 1945, completely implemented any of Beveridge's plans. But governments did select and modify objectives and instruments of policy which Beveridge powerfully advocated in his major texts. The report on *Social Insurance and the Allied Services (SIAS)* in 1942, for example, defined the shape of the British social security system for a generation after 1945. Our object, therefore, is the philosophic ghost which haunts the policy machine.

If this book proposes a new reading of Beveridge's collectivism, it is necessary to begin by indicating how and why our reading of Beveridge is different. In an earlier generation, the social administration texts of authors like Vic George (1968) or Jim Kincaid (1973) said many sensible things about the limits of Beveridge-style social insurance. But now more than twenty years after his death and more than forty years after his classic reports of the 1940s, the assessment of Beveridge has mostly passed into the hands of the historians. The more recent historical analyses of Beveridge's collectivism contain, in our view, arguments and conclusions which are in the end misleading. All the historians who write about Beveridge's collectivism start from the sensible premise that it was not always the same; his collectivism of 1909 is obviously different from his collectivism of the 1940s. But the nature of Beveridge's early and late collectivism is not satisfactorily defined in the existing historical accounts and consequently the break between 'young Beveridge' and 'old Beveridge' is mis-specified. In this brief introduction it is not possible to survey all of the historical literature on Beveridge. But it is possible to analyse the nature of the misunderstanding about his collectivism by examining two of the most serious recent historical accounts of Beveridge. The Edwardian collectivism of Beveridge is defined in Freeden's 1978 book *The New Liberalism* which appraises Beveridge in the context of advanced liberal opinion in the 1900s. The collectivism of Beveridge in the 1940s is defined in Harris's 1977 biography of Beveridge which provides a substantial account of his writings of the 1940s. Freeden presents the Edwardian Beveridge as a right-wing technician of an illiberal kind, while Harris emphasizes the ambition and scope of Beveridge's left, quasi-socialist collectivism in the 1940s. In outline, this book argues that Beveridge in the 1900s was not as far to the right as Freeden makes out and that Beveridge in the 1940s was not as far to the left as Harris makes out. In the reminder of this introduction, we will analyse how and why Freeden and Harris, in our view, misrepresent Beveridge.

The Freeden approach to Beveridge's 1909 text *Unemployment* ends up by, so to speak, charging Beveridge with three offences. First, Freeden alleges that Beveridge's project of reorganizing the labour market through the introduction of labour exchanges and unemployment insurance was illiberal and authoritarian (Freeden, 1978, pp. 184–5). The plan was to concentrate available employment on some of the underemployed casuals in a way that would create a visible surplus population for whom emigration and/or some form of protective custody would be appropriate. The second charge against Beveridge is that he lacked a broad perspective on general social welfare and social justice in the community. In 1909 Beveridge abstracted the problem of unemployment from this broader context.

> Beveridge dealt with the problem of unemployment very much in detachment from other crucial issues of social reform, with little consideration for the totality of human needs ... It was for him more a question of organising a specific sub-system than one of the individual welfare of all the members of society. (Freeden, 1978, pp. 210–11)

The third and final charge is that Beveridge in *Unemployment* displayed an aversion to the radical theories which had already been developed by such 'advanced' liberal writers as J. A. Hobson[1] and L. T. Hobhouse.[2] It is partly because of Beveridge's rejection of the possibility of underconsumption that the notion of redistribution does not figure at all in his analysis (Freeden, 1978, p. 211).

In appraising these criticisms it is important to remember that Freeden's object in *The New Liberalism* is the reformulation of liberalism by an avant-garde of 'advanced liberals' like Hobson and Hobhouse. Freeden appropriately applies an intellectual standard to the task of determining who is or is not a liberal. But he chooses to apply what may be called the Hobson standard to Edwardian writers; only those who are equally advanced intellectually can be enrolled as New Liberals. This is not the place to attempt a definition of liberalism and it must, in any case, be doubtful whether that changing creed has any simple essential identity. From our point of view, it is enough to demonstrate that, while Hobson and Hobhouse represented a left variant on liberalism, Beveridge represented an equally legitimate right variant. Thus we would argue that the Hobson standard of liberalism should be rejected as a sole criterion; it is altogether too severe and the resulting demarcation of Beveridge as illiberal is thoroughly uninformative:

Factually, Freeden is correct about Beveridge's position on the residuum of 'unemployables'; in 1909 Beveridge did conclude that 'the inefficient cannot safely be left at large to bring up in semi-starvation fresh generations of inefficients' (*Unemployment*, 1909, p. 204). Beveridge did later talk about what the German Nazis did after 1933 when they instituted a system of protective custody for 'volksgenossen' or fellow countrymen 'who deliberately ignore their duties towards the community' (Distel, 1978, p. 42). And such systems can only be created at the expense of an illiberal abridgement of citizen rights. But if an enthusiasm for protective custody disqualifies Edwardian social reformers from being liberal (or socialist), then there were no liberal or socialist intellectuals in England at this time. All of them, including Hobson (see Freeden, 1978, p. 178), regrettably fail this test. In this case the really significant issue is what else Edwardians like Beveridge proposed because that is the only practical basis for demarcating the liberals from the rest.

From this point of view it is important that most of the rest of Beveridge's proposals could be and were taken up and developed in a liberal problematic. The whole strategy and several technical elements in Beveridge's 1909 proposals reflected a liberal philosophy of the radical right. The project of reorganizing the labour market through labour exchanges and eliminating the 'hawking of labour' was one for perfecting the labour market as a liberal institution; as Chapter 4 shows, Beveridge tellingly described the project as one of 'making reality correspond with the assumptions of economic theory'. The proposal for social insurance to bridge occasional spells of cyclical unemployment was positive in that it put income maintenance on a contractual basis with the citizen gaining a limited right to benefit in return for contributions, whilst, in a negative sense, it helped to make tutelage or supervision of the population unnecessary. Furthermore, the liberalism of Beveridge's proposals was reinforced in the process of partial implementation when the Liberal government introduced labour exchanges and unemployment insurance after 1909. The key point here is that labour exchanges were introduced but never used for decasualization as Beveridge had originally proposed; notification of vacancies by employers was always voluntary and, without compulsory notification, a policy of decasualization was always impossible.

Freeden's argument comes to a paradoxical conclusion; Beveridge whose views do not qualify as liberal turns out to be 'the liberal who most influenced the Liberal cabinet' (Freeden, 1978, p. 10) while Hobson who was 'the most original and penetrating' new liberal theorist failed to influence Liberal party or government policy (Freeden, 1978, pp. 254, 256). This paradox can be resolved if we accept that the Edwardian Beveridge developed a kind of right liberalism which could be easily turned into practical policies. The device of social insurance, like the voluntary labour exchange, was a technical fix with liberal credentials which was easy to implement exactly because it did not require elaborate corollary policies or large-scale redistribution of income as proposed by the 'advanced liberals'. In his later work Beveridge advances on to the terrain opened up by these techniques. From the early 1920s he is advocating the extension of social insurance and the contract of income maintenance. And by the early 1940s he is more broadly engaged in defining the terms on which purchasing power can be regulated so that individuals can secure a subsistence standard of living and society can secure full employment. At one point Freeden observes that the social reformer's task is 'providing workable solutions to the critical social political problems of the times' (Freeden, 1978, p. 248).

By this standard it was 'new liberalism' exemplified by Hobson and Hobhouse which turned out to be a cul-de-sac, whilst the decisive influence on the modernization of social policy was exerted by a right liberalism which Beveridge exemplifies and develops.

The Harris biography of Beveridge is exactly that; it is a life of Beveridge produced by a historian whose forte is social administration. But Harris does accept that it is necessary to characterize Beveridge's ideas and one of the avowed aims of the book is to 'analyse the underlying assumptions of Beveridge's social philosophy' (Harris, 1977, p. 2). She represents Beveridge as someone who veered rather incoherently between individualism and collectivism.

> Between 1900 and 1942 there was scarcely a point on the compass of liberal philosophy through which he did not travel, and at times he went far beyond the bounds of what is conventionally thought of as 'liberalism'. Far from being a consistent 'welfare collectivist' he veered between an almost total commitment to the free market and an equally strong commitment to an authoritarian administrative state. At times he favoured generous social welfare and radical redistribution of resources; but at other times he favoured 'the whip of starvation as a necessary precondition of economic advance'. (Harris, 1977, p. 2)

Harris distinguishes three chronological phases and two transitions in Beveridge's thought (Harris, 1977, pp. 471–2). In a first transition radical youth gave way to cautious middle age in the interwar period and in a second transition radicalism is reasserted in old age as Beveridge in the 1940s became an ambitious collectivist who wished to extend the sphere of state action in a massive way. In this final period, Beveridge

> came to the conclusion that the so-called free market had irretrievably broken down; and he pressed again for far-reaching measures of state intervention – this time not merely in social welfare but in running the economy. (Harris, 1977, p. 472)

Beveridge's intellectual development from the 1930s to the 1940s is therefore constructed as a move from individualism to collectivism. And Beveridge of the 1940s is represented as the prophet of 'a highly collectivist planned society' (Harris, 1977, p. 440).

Many of the confusions in this account arise because collectivism

7

exists as an unexamined category in the Harris book. Indeed, in her discussion of the 1940s period, Harris tends towards a sociological rather than an intellectual definition of collectivism. Thus, she argues that

> in terms of social and economic policy Beveridge's views between 1942 and 1944 were virtually indistinguishable from those of many people in the Labour party who called themselves socialists. On questions such as public ownership, redistribution of income and extension of social services he did not fundamentally disagree with socialist politicians like Aneurin Bevan and Stafford Cripps. (Harris, 1977, p. 440)

Leaving aside the question of whether there was a collectivist lib-lab alliance in the 1940s, the problem of course is how to characterize the identity of these 'views'. Harris cannot satisfactorily analyse Beveridge's final position for two reasons. First, she constructs an intertext which includes only the progressive, collectivist texts of the 1940s, principally *Social Insurance and the Allied Services (SIAS)* in 1942 and *Full Employment in a Free Society* in 1944. She relegates to marginality the reactionary individualist texts of the 1940s, principally *Voluntary Action* (1948) and *Evidence for Voluntary Action* (1948). Fifty pages of the biography are devoted to *SIAS* but *Voluntary Action* is dismissed in just over one page (Harris, 1977, pp. 458–9) in a chapter on Beveridge's old age and then rather elliptically referred to again in the conclusion (Harris, pp. 472–6). The second major problem is that when Harris reads Beveridge's texts she applies a simple 'either individualism or collectivism' grid. At best this approach can only weight the elements of individualism and collectivism before determining whether a text is individualist or collectivist. The result is a kind of yes/no, tick-the-box approach to classifying positions on state intervention.

Harris's own choice of texts hardly proves her thesis about the ambition and scope of Beveridge's collectivism in the 1940s. Two classic reports, *SIAS* of 1942 and *Full Employment* of 1944, feature in the Harris biography. But, as the readings in this volume show, these reports recommend that minimalist techniques of state welfare should be used to achieve limited liberal objectives. Full employment and the abolition of poverty were radical objectives in the 1940s but they were not distinctively socialist. Indeed Beveridge's strategy could be represented as a right liberal substitute for socialism because he proposed levelling up the poor to minimum standards of income and security without any levelling down of the rich. On the question of techniques, Beveridge was attracted by Keynesian demand management exactly because it promised to deliver full employment without the need for more dirigiste forms of planning which would curtail the freedom of capitalist owners and managers; planning of this more radical kind was to be kept in reserve and used only if Keynesianism failed. As for social insurance, that was to be developed on the basis of flat rate contributions and benefits with no means tests. Beveridge quite explicitly supported this kind of social insurance because it created a minimum of interference with the individual's freedom to spend his own income and make additional 'voluntary provision'. In this context Harris's neglect of the *Voluntary Action* (1948) book is particularly unfortunate. Beveridge correctly identified this book as a sequel 'third report' which followed on from the two earlier reports; the work is even structured in the same way with one volume of analysis supported by one volume of evidence. The analysis is concerned with the form and extent of 'voluntary' provision in a full employment welfare state. Beveridge argued that this expansion of state activity need not result in a withering away of non-state activity; there could and should be an expansion of private welfare services provided by voluntary associations like the friendly societies which had long offered sickness insurance. *Voluntary Action* does not fit the historical stereotype of arch-collectivist Beveridge. Perhaps that partly explains why it is mostly ignored.

Beyond this, the texts which are included in the Harris account are misrepresented inadvertently because she uses the two poles concept of individualism or collectivism. This suppresses the fundamental point that Beveridge's position of the 1940s is defined by the way in which he combines elements of individualism and collectivism to produce a result which we term 'liberal collectivism'. Beveridge powerfully developed this *a priori* in the 1940s by specifying a new set of economic and social policy instruments and objectives adequate to the political philosophy. That is the landmark significance of the 1942 and 1944 reports on the abolition of poverty through social insurance and the attainment of full employment through demand management. But the *a priori* was first developed in the policy field by Harold Macmillan in *The Middle Way* (1937).[3] And Macmillan's text provides the best introduction to its general characteristics because in this earlier work the difference between liberal collectivism and socialist collectivism is very clearly defined. The central problem of the Harris account is that her approach cannot leave space for the possibility of a distinctive non-socialist collectivism which retains many of the premises and objectives of traditional individualism.

Liberal collectivism starts from the position that state intervention is absolutely necessary. Macmillan, like later liberal collectivists, emphasized that the free market generated and would never resolve problems like poverty and economic insecurity. Thus some kind of state social security, for example, was absolutely necessary. But the question was where and how the line about state intervention should be drawn. Liberal collectivism proposed a distinctive non-socialist answer to this question because it argued that state intervention could and should be minimal in two ways. First, state intervention should be minimal because it could be limited and confined to what was necessary. This minimalism differentiates liberal and socialist collectivists in the debates about planning in the 1930s. Socialist collectivists, like Durbin (1940), argued that planning should be used to reduce inequality through a series of policies which addressed the whole range of top to bottom income inequalities. Liberal collectivists like Macmillan argued that planning should be used only to eliminate poverty, that is, to bring those on low incomes up to a minimum standard. Secondly, state intervention should be minimal because there should be as little interference as possible with the valuable political and economic freedoms of capitalism. This is another point of difference between liberal and socialist collectivists. Socialist collectivists have always disparaged the formal freedoms of capitalism which leave the doors of the Ritz equally open to the rich and the poor. On the other hand, liberal collectivists value capitalist freedoms and have always been concerned to design forms of state intervention which safeguard these freedoms. Classically, liberal collectivists have argued that, with state regulation or action established in one sphere of the economy, unregulated market choice can flourish elsewhere. Thus Macmillan in the 1930s argued that, after state co-operatives had taken over the supply of basic necessities, the production of fur coats, gramophones and slim volumes of poetry should take place on market principles.

The new liberal position was distinctive and non-socialist because it recommended large slabs of collectivism in the interests of preserving as much as possible of capitalist individualism. The liberal collectivists (as we have dubbed them) accepted the traditional philosophical justification of capitalism as a political and economic system whose virtue was that it left a man free to do what he willed with his own. At the same time, the liberal collectivists believed that the consequences of this freedom on and for the market were entirely unacceptable and that these consequences would have to be curbed by state intervention in some respects if capitalist freedoms were to survive more generally. To make these points more positively, it could be said that the liberal collectivists seductively promised the best of both worlds; capitalist freedoms would flourish in a new order which suppressed capitalist problems as effectively as the socialism which abridged these freedoms.

We would not, of course, deny that the introduction of new policy instruments and objectives after 1945 had material preconditions; prosaic techniques like the PAYE system for cumulative withholding of income tax from current income helped make Keynesian demand management possible. The point about material preconditions has been well developed by Tomlinson (1981). But the ideological promise of the best of both worlds did help make Beveridge's novelties into the first principles of postwar economic and social policy. When the postwar policy settlement has failed us, no one can now believe in that promise of a capitalist full employment welfare state. And some pretend to know why the instruments of demand management and social insurance can never achieve their objectives. But there has been an extraordinary lack of interest in the political philosophy which was inherent in the new policy instruments and objectives. One of the aims of this book is to initiate a long-overdue debate on the nature and limits of that political philosophy.

CHAPTER

1

The Economic and Social Philosophy of 'A Free Society'

Beveridge was never a grand social theorist. As the titles of his books and articles show, he always favoured a practical problem-centred approach to specific issues. He was writing *Unemployment: a problem of industry* (1909) in the years when his Edwardian contemporaries Hobhouse and Hobson were writing books on *Liberalism* (1911) and *The Crisis of Liberalism* (1909). Towards the end of his career, in 1945, some of his journalism was collected into a short book titled *Why I am a Liberal*. But the contents of that book only prove our point about practical preoccupation because this was not a text of political theory; in its introduction Beveridge explained 'why I have joined the Liberal party' and in its conclusion argued 'why you should vote Liberal in the 1945 general election. It would, however, be wrong to represent Beveridge as a mere technician of social reform who was belatedly converted to party politics. Beveridge always occupied a position which was in some sense liberal and in his work of the 1930s and 1940s his underlying political philosophy was increasingly formalized and elaborated. From this point of view our main interest must be to define Beveridge's positions and examine their development.

Even by the standards of problem-centred Edwardian writers, Beveridge's pre-1914 work was remarkably untheoretical. He produced nothing like Rowntree's[1] book on *The Land Question* which both rested upon and investigated a radical theory of property. And the treatment of theoretical issues which Beveridge could not avoid,

12

like Hobson's[2] theory of underconsumption, was flaccid and unconvincing. But, of course, the world is such that those with an inferior theoretical formation and worse arguments often have more influence, and Beveridge's success illustrates that point. We disagree with Freeden about the nature of this influence; Beveridge in the 1900s was less philosophical and well to the right of advanced new liberals like Hobson whose demands for redistribution were grounded in radical economics and a liberal political theory of citizenship. But, as we have argued, that does not make him any less of a liberal. The central proposal of *Unemployment* for 'reorganization of the labour market' was designed to perfect the working of a liberal institution and finally make reality correspond with economic theory. The corollary policy of insurance was less distinctively liberal but was, in practical terms, crucial exactly because it inaugurated a very limited redistribution of income which was politically acceptable to a broad range of opinion. This latter part of Beveridge's original programme constituted immediately feasible politics and the principle of insurance could then be extended so that, as Chapters 2 and 3 show, this technique of welfare became the cornerstone of the British system of income maintenance. The extracts in these later chapters show that, by the 1940s, Beveridge was well aware that insurance rested on the liberal principle of a contract between the individual and the state which offered maintenance in exchange for contributions.

Beveridge's position of the 1900s is mainly of interest therefore because it represents a right liberal position which is capable of development within the mainstream of British politics. Indeed, Beveridge's achievement was that he redirected this mainstream after 1945 through his development and articulation of the right-wing liberal position in the 1930s and 1940s. The extracts in this chapter are designed to illustrate that development over these two crucial decades when Beveridge was converted to liberal collectivism. The first extract (1A) is taken from his economic writings of the mid 1930s and illustrates a kind of intellectual blockage; in 1935 Beveridge could not see how planned capitalism offered a 'third way' and might be preferable to either unregulated capitalism or socialism. Subsequent extracts (1B, C and D) from the two classic reports of the 1940s on full employment and social insurance illustrate Beveridge's conversion to a new and rather different kind of planning than that which he had earlier criticized. These extracts also demonstrate the character of Beveridge's mature and increasingly explicit political philosophy; liberal collectivism underpins the proposals for minimal state intervention to abolish poverty and unemployment. The final extract (1E) is taken from the neglected and unread third Beveridge report, on voluntary action. It gives us Beveridge's distinctive final view on the nature of a 'free society' where the business motive would be restrained and an altruistic voluntary sector would play a major role.

In the 1930s Beveridge began to discuss the broad choice between capitalism and socialism for the first time in a serious and fluent way. His lectures and journalism of this period form a commentary on the 1930s discussion of planning. Like many contemporaries Beveridge was at first attracted by the concept of a planned capitalist economy which would be a kind of 'halfway house' between a centrally regulated socialist economy and a capitalist market economy:

> Most people are looking for a compromise between free prices and planning – for a halfway house between Cobden and Lenin; they want planning in part, without going the whole way to Russia. (extract 1A)

The political orientation of the planning project in the 1930s was epitomized by the dust-jacket design of Harold Macmillan's[3] 1937 book *The Middle Way* where the title appeared between the hammer and sickle on the left and *fasces* on the right: Beveridge's appraisal of this project in the 1930s was determined by Von Mises's[4] criticism of all socialist planning which abridged the allocation of resources through the price mechanism. These arguments about the necessary inefficiency of a centrally regulated socialist economy were domesticated for English consumption by academics like Hayek[5] and Robbins[6] who taught at the LSE where Beveridge was director. Beveridge simply observed that the arguments against 'complete socialism' could be extended and applied to planned capitalism.

> In so far as planning under capitalism means monopolies, partial or complete . . . competition is prevented from executing the judgements delivered by the pricing process [and] the doubts raised by economists against the efficiency of socialism apply to planned capitalism with equal force. (extract 1A)

Beveridge's economic doubts about discarding 'the pricing process as governor of production' were reinforced by political doubts about whether planning could be made to work without the abridgement of 'essential liberties'.

At the same time, it should be emphasized that Beveridge in the 1930s was never a right-wing apologist for the market economy. He recognized that if socialism or planned capitalism would be inefficient, free market capitalism had not delivered full employment because labour and capital were everywhere idle. Unregulated capitalism was caught in a kind of double bind because the pricing mechanism which promoted an efficient allocation of resources also generated economic depression:

> the pricing process necessarily works through money, and money in advanced capitalist countries, taking the form of credit, has got out of hand. As a consequence, all such countries suffer from recurrent inflations followed by depressions, in which a large proportion of the means of production, so far from being used to best advantage in yielding welfare, is not used at all. (extract 1A)

Beveridge's position of the mid 1930s was one of agnosticism; he could not conceive of any kind of economic system which would deliver an efficient allocation of resources and full employment. This defeatist conclusion was inevitable in the economic problematic within which he was working. Intervention within a capitalist economy was equated with forms of planning which abridged the price mechanism necessary to efficiency and cyclical problems were attributed to problems about credit which was a form of money necessary to advanced capitalist economies. Within the circle of these assumptions it was not possible to sustain positive and progressive conclusions.

The emergence of Keynesianism in the early 1940s liberated Beveridge. Keynes's *General Theory* in 1936 had identified demand deficiency as a cause of unemployment and had proposed the solution of stabilizing investment expenditure through the 'socialization of investment'. If this was technically and politically difficult, Keynes in his 1940 pamphlet *How to Pay for the War* suggested that consumption expenditure could be manipulated through fiscal policy. And, if the immediate problem was to deal with wartime excess demand, fiscal policy could also be adopted to deal with demand deficiency. At this point Keynesianism and a new concept of economic management (rather than planning) were born. Beveridge's own conversion to Keynes and Keynesianism can be dated fairly precisely from his journalism of 1942 and 1943, which was collected together and published in a volume entitled *Pillars of Security and Other Wartime Essays and Addresses*. The 1942 report on social insurance identified 'the avoidance of mass unemployment' as a precondition for the successful operation of social security (extract 1D). But, in December 1942 when the report was published, Beveridge admitted he did not know how this end might be achieved.

> I simply do not believe that it is impossible to abolish unemployment in Britain; but I do not yet know exactly how it ought to be done, and I don't know whether anybody yet knows how it ought to be done. (*Pillars of Security*, 1943, p. 88)

By March 1943 Beveridge wrote altogether more confidently: 'I do not believe there is the slightest reason why we should have as much unemployment' as the 10 per cent assumed by the government actuary in costing the 1942 report (*Pillars of Security*, 1943, p. 140). A broadcast on 'the prevention of unemployment' in October 1943 demonstrated that the new optimism had a coherent theoretical basis (Beveridge on Beveridge 1944, pp. 36–40). 'The direction in which we should look for a solution' was the work of Keynes which contained the insight that the level of employment is determined by the level of spending by consumers, businesses and government. For full employment, 'the sum total of all these separate spendings must be such as to set up a demand for all the labour and other productive resources of the community'. Even if the policy implications are blurred, this broadcast marks the point of Beveridge's conversion to Keynes, with Keynesianism to follow when he had worked out the policy implications of his new position.

The break of 1943 opened up the economic terrain of liberal collectivism which Beveridge advanced to occupy in his second major report, on *Full Employment in a Free Society*, published in 1944. As the title suggests, the discussion of the technically economic is in this report integrated with a broader economic and social philosophy. This point emerges very clearly if we consider the prime objective of full employment. This target is defined in technical economic terms as 'not more than 3 per cent unemployment' (extract 1B). But the goal is not simply a technical one because Beveridge insists that it is only worthwhile if it can be achieved in a liberal capitalist political context. This context is specified in terms of a list of 'essential liberties' which must be preserved.

For the purpose of this Report they are taken as freedom of worship, speech, writing, study and teaching; freedom of assembly and of association for political and other purposes, including the bringing about of a peaceful change of the governing authority; freedom in choice of occupation; and freedom in the management of a personal income. (extract 1B)

The existence of such liberties defines the non-totalitarian 'free society' with democratic politics, free trade unions and consumer sovereignty. The list of political liberties is in one respect interesting because Beveridge explicitly excludes 'private ownership of means of production' on the grounds that this liberty 'never has been enjoyed by more than a very small proportion of the British people' (extract 1B). Beveridge characterizes private ownership of the means of production as an 'economic device' (extract 1B). But this heresy is less significant than it first appears because by 1944 Beveridge is convinced that liberal collectivist economic policies can in practice deliver full employment without encroaching on private ownership of the means of production. Even so, the point would have to be conceded that in *Full Employment in a Free Society* Beveridge carried acceptance of intervention to the very limits of compatability with liberal collectivism. His conviction that full employment had become a necessary condition for the stability of democratic liberalism forced him to re-examine and recategorize the fundamental freedoms. Private property was not questioned but private ownership of the means of production was seen to be a 'secondary' freedom. This was because Beveridge then thought it might occasionally be necessary to interfere with private ownership in order to maintain full employment (e.g. to implement a policy of regional development). The concession was, however, only to permit, and then only if it should prove necessary, such intervention as was required for a minimalist management of an essentially capitalist economy.

If Marx had put the comprehensive socialization of production on to the socialist agenda, Keynes put the selective socialization of demand on to a new liberal collectivist agenda. *Full Employment* illustrates Beveridge's conversion to the new minimalist 'policy . . . of socializing demand rather than production' (extract 1C).

The policy set out here is one which might be adopted by a community which held firmly to private enterprise, and accepted the principle laid down by an American economist: 'Private industry can and will do the job

17

of production. It is the responsibility of the Government to do its part to ensure a constant demand.'. . . . There is every reason for hoping that full employment could be secured in place by the policy outlined here, while leaving the major part of industry to private enterprise. (extract 1C)

Beveridge did carefully reserve the right to encroach further upon the liberties of capitalists and workers. Effective socialization of demand might require selective nationalization and regulation of the investment plans of large private corporations. Furthermore, the state should intervene to curb any abuse of privilege by private business or trade unions in a full employment economy. But Beveridge's hope was that a minimalist economic policy would be sufficient.

Beveridge's first major report of the 1940s, on *Social Insurance and the Allied Services* in 1942, rested on the assumption of 'the avoidance of mass unemployment'. Beveridge's liberal collectivism was rounded and complete only when he specified how this objective would be achieved in the second report of 1944 on *Full Employment*. Nevertheless, in the sphere of the social, Beveridge had already worked out a liberal collectivist strategy in the 1942 report. *SIAS* is a tour de force because the design of the social insurance scheme is at every stage subordinated to the requirements of the liberal *a priori*. A fuller demonstration of this point is reserved for the next chapter of this reader. But extract 1D in this chapter should in a preliminary way establish the liberal collectivist paternity of the strategy.

The first step is to clear away Beveridge's misrepresentation of the political pertinence of his social insurance scheme. As scientists must try to understand their discoveries, so social reformers must try to interpret their reform strategies. In both cases, the accounts may be misleading because intellectuals do not know, or do not want to know, what they are doing. Beveridge's own account of the political pertinence of his social insurance scheme in 1942 was disingenuous for the best of reasons. To improve chances of implementation on a bipartisan basis he repeatedly insisted that 'the plan raises no party issues' (*Pillars of Security*, 1943, p. 77). To reinforce this point, he also claimed that the plan was politically neutral at a more philosophical level. In a popular exposition of the newly published report, he used the argument that the technique of social insurance was required under both capitalism and socialism:

the Plan is a move neither towards Socialism nor towards Capitalism. It

18

goes straight down the middle of the road between them to a practical end. It is needed in any form of economic organization. (*Pillars of Security*, 1943, p. 77)

Of course, the technique of social insurance can be, and has been, used in socialist societies for financing old age pensions and other income maintenance. But, as we have already noted, social insurance does establish a congenially liberal principle of contract between the individual and the state. And from the early 1920s, in Beveridge's proposals for social insurance, the contract was always set up so that it secured liberal rather than socialist objectives. A socialist-inspired contract would have had at its centre such aims as using social insurance to effect a substantial redistribution of income to obtain a more equitable society. Beveridge's liberal collectivist intention showed through in the rejection of such aims and in the conditional offer of income subvention at a minimal level. In a section of a 1924 pamphlet headed 'insurance or communism', this issue was discussed in a clear and honest way.

> The problem is not that of guaranteeing an income at all times to every-body irrespective of his work and services. That way lies Communism. The problem is the narrower one of giving security against all the main risks of economic life to those who depend on continuous earning, of arranging that part of what such persons earn by their work shall take the form of provision for themselves and their dependants whenever their work is interrupted or stopped by causes beyond their control. This is the line of social insurance, maintaining individual freedom and responsibilities and the family as the unit of the State. (*Insurance for All and Everything*, 1924, p. 31)

In Beveridge's writings on insurance the liberal political objectives were always to be achieved by establishing some form of limit on the claimant's entitlement to benefit. The development in his thought over thirty years comes from the way in which the nature of this limitation is rethought. In the 1924 pamphlet, *Insurance for All and Everything*, the limit is still to be established in the Edwardian way through the payment of relatively low allowances and time limits on the drawing of unemployment benefit. By 1942 in *SIAS* these particular limits are suspended. As extract 1D shows, the 1942 report proposed a benefit which would be 'sufficient without further resources to provide the minimum income needed for subsistence in all normal cases' and such benefits would 'continue indefinitely without means test, so long as the need continues'. But this progressive change was possible only because social insurance had been inserted into the new minimalism of liberal collectivism which retained some of the old limits and also established new ones. The general definition of social security in 1942 remained minimalist because social security was equated with income maintenance for those who were temporarily or permanently unwaged.

> The term 'social security' is used here to denote the securing of an income to take the place of earnings when they are interrupted by unemployment, sickness or accident, to provide for retirement through age, to provide against loss of support by the death of another person, and to meet exceptional expenditures, such as those connected with birth, death and marriage. (extract 1D)

In this kind of social security scheme, there was to be a minimum of interference with the wages contract and the labour market; under the 1942 proposals the low paid would benefit only through child allowances which would be paid to waged and unwaged alike so as not to interfere with incentives. More specifically the generous proposal to pay substantially increased 'adequate benefits' was coherent with the new liberal collectivist minimalism about safeguarding the basic conditions of social life without encroaching unnecessarily on the market. The 1942 report offered 'security of income up to a minimum' and not a penny more; that was the logic of the proposal for 'a flat rate' of subsistence benefit which was one of the six major principles of 1942.

In another way, the *SIAS* proposals of 1942 were also liberal collectivist because they were designed to re-establish the conditions for capitalist freedom elsewhere, outside the enlarged sphere of state activity. As extract 1D shows, flat rate insurance benefits were recommended because they provided an incentive for individuals to make additional private provision.

> This principle follows from the recognition of the place and importance of voluntary insurance in social security. (extract 1D)

The 1942 Social Insurance Report did not analyse the form which private provision would and should take. This was the prime object of analysis in Beveridge's third report of 1948 which examined how 'voluntary action' should adjust to the enlargement of state activity previously proposed.

The liberal collectivist credo was resolutely stated in this third report.

> It is clear that the State must in future do more things than it has attempted in the past. But it is equally clear, or should be equally clear, that room, opportunity and encouragement must be kept for voluntary action in seeking new ways of social advance. (*Voluntary Action*, 1948, p. 10)

The emphasis on 'voluntary action' shows how Beveridge had by 1948 moved beyond a classic liberal collectivism which sets up a polar opposition between the state and the market while posing the problem of where the line between the state and the market should be drawn. By the third report in 1948, this simple analysis is being displaced because Beveridge is insisting that voluntary action does and should function as a kind of necessary buffer zone between the state and the market. This position was implicit in Beveridge's defence of mutual insurance against sickness through the medium of non-profit-making friendly societies.[7]

> It would be a pity if the whole field of security against misfortune, once the domain of voluntary Mutual Aid, became divided between the State and private business conducted for gain. (*Voluntary Action*, 1948, p. 294)

Like many other writers of the 1940s, Beveridge treated 'the business motive' which sustained the market with considerable disdain.

> The business motive is a good servant but a bad master, and a society which gives itself up to the dominance of the business motive is a bad society. (extract 1E)

Voluntary action could provide an altruistic counterweight to selfishness because the dominant motives of voluntary action were 'mutual aid' and 'philanthropy'. Institutions of voluntary action like trade unions, co-operative stores, friendly societies, building societies and so forth were all credited with these motives. They represented 'private enterprise, not in business but in the service of mankind, not for gain but under the driving power of social conscience' (*Voluntary Action*, 1948, p. 322). For high moral reasons the growth of voluntary action should therefore be encouraged by the state.

The expansion of state activity need not threaten voluntary action because under a new division of labour the voluntary sector could concentrate on the provision of 'services' while the state redistributed expenditure through guaranteeing social security and promoting full employment (extract 1E). According to Beveridge, voluntary action did not necessarily rely on unpaid workers or uphold the principle of voluntary association and free choice of membership. The defining characteristic of voluntary action was its 'independence from public control' (*Voluntary Action*, 1948, p. 8): that is, the agencies undertaking voluntary action were not under the direction of any authority wielding the power of the state. The existence of self-regulating and self-governing voluntary action associations was therefore politically important because it demarcated a free democratic society from a 'totalitarian society' where trade unions, co-ops and friendly societies were all state-controlled.

> In a totalitarian society, all action outside the citizen's home is directed or controlled by the state. By contrast, vigour and abundance of Voluntary Action outside one's home, individually and in association with other citizens, for bettering one's own life and that of one's fellows, are the distinguishing marks of a free society. (*Voluntary Action*, 1948, p. 10)

By the late 1940s, Beveridge had developed a coherent and distinctive liberal collectivist philosophy. The state should accept a responsibility for full employment and provide adequate maintenance for the unwaged. These objectives could hopefully be achieved without encroaching on liberal freedoms in a capitalist society where the operation of market forces would be naturally humanized by voluntary action for higher motives. This conclusion raises interesting questions about Beveridge's shifts of position which prepared the way for his mature liberal collectivism and these issues are analysed in Chapters 3 and 4 of this reader, on unemployment and the development of social insurance as a technique of welfare. Our conclusion also raises more political questions about the limits of Beveridge's philosophy. An economic and social philosophy of this kind can be criticized in two ways. It can be argued that the philosophy must fail because it is inherently flawed. Or, alternatively, it can be argued that the philosophy must fail because there is a fatal discrepancy between the world as it exists and the world as it is ideologically preconstructed. Both lines of criticism are taken up in later chapters of this reader, especially in Chapters 2 and 5 on *SIAS* and *Voluntary Action*.

1A   'Between Cobden and Lenin' – the Dilemmas of Planning in the 1930s

Source: Planning under Socialism (1936), pp. 7–9, 26–30, 107–9

(The first and third extracts here are taken from a 1935 lecture on 'the economic implications of planning under socialism' and the second is taken from a radio talk on 'prices and planning' which was given in the same year. Beveridge published both addresses in a collection brought out in 1936.)

Consider the claim made for the pricing process under capitalism. The consumer having £1 in his pocket, to spend or not as he likes, makes a decision in favour (say) of boots rather than books made by a particular process or maker rather than by another, of boots now rather than books or some other satisfaction later. He judges his own welfare, as no one else can, and, to the limit of £1, directs the whole economic system to serve his welfare.

There is no denying the merits of this type of governor. Its advocates can claim, moreover, that it has stood the test of experience; it is not a new-fangled toy. It has been used for centuries by all the best peoples, and, broadly speaking, its users have grown steadily richer.

Yet, equally, it has certain disadvantages. I shall name three only.

First, the pricing process necessarily works through money, and money in advanced capitalist countries, taking the form of credit, has got out of hand. As a consequence, all such countries suffer from recurrent inflations followed by depressions, in which a large proportion of the means of production, so far from being used to best advantage in yielding welfare, is not used at all.

Second, capitalism, guided by the pricing process, has led to great inequalities of individual income. It cannot fairly be denied that this is a disadvantage, on the ground that the last half-crown in a

23

dustman's pocket normally satisfies more urgent wants than the last half-crown of the millionaire . . .

Third, the private ownership of the means of production, which is essential to the pricing process, tends to throw into antagonistic camps those upon whose continuing co-operation production depends – that is to say, the managers of industry and the workmen.

Having prices and markets for everything is one way – at present the commonest way – of determining just how much of everything is wanted and who can best produce it, of bringing about the right division of labour.

It isn't, of course, the only possible way of doing this and it isn't a perfect way. The economic system obviously isn't working perfectly today. So far from demand and supply getting neatly adjusted everywhere by changing market prices, there seem to be everywhere unsatisfied demands and unused supplies, men and machines standing idle and other men wanting, but unable to pay for, the things that the idle men could make.

Some people say that's because the price and market system under which we have lived in the past is a hopelessly bad system; they want to scrap it and replace it by a completely planned system, like the Russian, trying to get the right division of labour, not automatically through prices, but by orders to everybody from a planning centre. They point out that by demand the economist and the grocer selling bacon always mean only demand backed by ability to pay – effective demand. That's a very different thing from human needs. They say that by complete planning one could secure for all people sufficient for their human needs and that this is more important than the kind of freedom which producers and consumers have today.

Other people say that the troubles of today arise, not because the price and market system itself is bad, but because we won't let it work as it was meant to work. They say it's an automatic device which should be left alone, it may not work perfectly but if you keep on fiddling with it, it can't work at all. These people would like to go back to less interference in business by Acts of Parliament.

Yet a third set of people think that you can combine prices and planning, so as to get the advantages of both, without the disadvantage of either.

That third set of people is the largest today. Most people are looking for a compromise between free prices and planning – for a halfway house between Cobden and Lenin; they want planning in part, without going the whole way to Russia. They do not want to abolish prices and markets and competition altogether, but want to regulate them and limit their action. The moral suggested to me from the experience of the milk dispute[8] and from many other experiments in State control is that this sort of compromise, though it is very attractive, is not at all easy. I do not say it is impossible, but it is not simple. You can't jab an Act of Parliament into the economic machine and stop one part of it – stop the free movement of market prices – and expect all the rest to go on as before. Once you begin to interfere, it's not easy to limit the extent of your interference. You may be driven much further towards complete planning than you meant to go when you started, or are certain to like when you get there.

The central problem of economics is the right division of labour . . . But economics doesn't tell you that you ought or ought not to fix prices by Act of Parliament; what it tells you is that if you do fix prices, instead of letting them rise and fall with the market, you will need some other method of keeping supply and demand in equilibrium and securing the right division of labour; any such method will mean limiting the freedom either of consumers or producers or of both. It is for the citizens of the country to say whether, knowing this, they will stick to free prices or try some other method.

The practical issue does not lie, and is never likely to lie, between planning under completed socialism and a free pricing process under capitalism. In practice we shall have to consider, on the one hand, proposals for partial socialism – the application of public ownership to some industries and not to others; on the other hand, proposals for planning under capitalism, that is to say for checking the free operation of the pricing process, without replacing the process completely. This does not mean that academic examination of completed socialism is irrelevant. Through that examination we have been led to see that the crucial question, under any form that completed socialism is likely to take in this country, is the price and production policy of monopolies: by what means, if at all, can that policy be made to conform to the general interest of securing the most productive use of available resources? The virtue of the pricing process under capitalism lies not in the private ownership of capital, but in the competition between those owners. In so far as planning under capitalism means monopolies, partial or complete, means that competition is prevented from executing the judgements delivered by the pricing process, the doubts raised by economists against the efficiency of socialism apply to planned capitalism with equal force. And most plans for planning under capitalism are of this type today: the talk is all of regulating markets, preventing loss of capital, restraining cut-throat competition, putting the power of the State behind monopolies and cartels . . . The world is too poor to afford economic mistakes. We cannot prudently discard the pricing process as governor of production, until we are satisfied both that a better new mechanism can be designed and that we shall be able to work it . . .

Any economic system that we choose must be such that politically we shall be able to work it. The economic implications of any proposal for the conduct of human affairs cannot be separated from its political implications. In the foregoing discussion, it has been convenient to compare the respective merits of rival devices for directing the division of labour, without looking beyond the devices themselves to the persons or authorities who would be required to operate them. I have assumed that each of these devices could and would be worked substantially as the makers intend. I have not, except once or twice in passing, looked beyond the machine itself, to consider what kind of political authority would be required to work it successfully, whether the establishment of such an authority could be counted on, what effect its establishment might have on the life of the citizens. This is suitable abstraction for the lecture-room. In real life, however, the technically best machine is of little value if the owner cannot work it; a fool- or knave-proof machine of lesser technical merit may be better worth having . . .

Before one decides to exchange the pricing process for planning under socialism, one must examine the political as well as the economic implications. In general terms, the problem is that of designing a governing authority whose mind is at once closed to propaganda and perpetually open to new ideas; which is democratic in the sense that it pursues the welfare of the people as welfare is understood by the people, and is unlike the government of any known democracy in being resistant to sectional pressures, and to passing gusts of popular opinion. Examination of this problem might lead to the conclusion that the technically most efficient economic machine was practically inferior, because calling for more political intelligence and honesty than could be guaranteed. It might appear impossible to set up a government capable of socialism, at least without risking essential liberties. It might appear, on the other hand, that working the pricing process required even greater intelligence and a self-restraint not to be hoped for either from democracies or from tyrants; there is plenty of evidence to support this opinion today.

The problem of completed socialism which I have put before you today, is not one which we can hope to solve by trial and error, or which we can trust to experiment. I have said nothing at all of the practical experiment of planning under State ownership of the means of production which is proceeding today in another country than our own. That is not because I believe that nothing at all is to be learned from Russia. My reason for saying nothing about Russia is, partly, that it is so hard to come at the truth there, and partly that any experience of that country can never be decisive for us. Failure of socialistic planning in Russia would not mean that success was impossible in a country with more experience of industry and longer experience of honest government. Success of socialistic planning in Russia would still leave open the question of the price in essential liberties at which it had been bought.

1B Full Employment with 'the Preservation of Essential Liberties'

Source: Full Employment in a Free Society (1944), pp. 21–4

Employment is not wanted for the sake of employment, irrespective of what it produces. The material end of all human activity is consumption. Employment is wanted as a means to more consumption or more leisure, as a means to a higher standard of life. Employment which is merely time-wasting, equivalent to digging holes and filling them again, or merely destructive, like war and preparing for war, will not serve that purpose. Nor will it be felt worth while. It must be productive and progressive. The proposals of this Report are designed to preserve all the essential springs of material progress in the community, to leave to special efforts its rewards, to leave scope for change, invention, competition and initiative.

In so far as room is left for change and for freedom of movement from job to job, room is left for some unemployment. The aim of this Report is expressed in numerical terms . . . as a reduction of unemployment to not more than 3 per cent, as compared with the 10 to 22 per cent experienced in Britain between the wars. But though the Report assumes the continuance of some unemployment and suggests a figure of 3 per cent, it is the essence of the proposals made in the Report that this 3 per cent should be unemployed only because there is industrial friction, and not because there are no vacant jobs. For men to have value and a sense of value there must always be useful things waiting to be done, with money to pay for doing them. Jobs, rather than men, should wait.

The labour market in the past has invariably, or all but invariably, been a buyer's market rather than a seller's market, with more unemployed men – generally many more unemployed men – than unfilled jobs. To reverse this and make the labour market always a seller's rather than a buyer's market, to remove not only unemployment but the fear of unemployment, would affect the working of many existing institutions. It would change and is meant to change fundamentally the conditions of living and working in Britain, to make Britain again a land of opportunity for all. There are some things in Britain which neither full employment nor the means of achieving it should be allowed to change.

The Report, as its title indicates, is not concerned simply with the problem of full employment. It is concerned with the necessity, possibility and methods of achieving full employment in a free society, that is to say, subject to the proviso that all essential citizen liberties are preserved. The precise effect of the proviso depends on the list of essential citizen liberties. For the purpose of this Report they are taken as freedom of worship, speech, writing, study and teaching; freedom of assembly and of association for political and other purposes, including the bringing about of a peaceful change of the governing authority; freedom in choice of occupation; and freedom in the management of a personal income. The proviso excludes the totalitarian solution of full employment in a society completely planned and regimented by an irremovable dictator. It makes the problem of full employment more complex in many ways, of which four call for special notice.

First, in a free society the governing authority is liable to be changed at short intervals by peaceful methods of political organization and voting. There must be reasonable continuity of economic policy in spite of such changes of government. The machinery of government, while responsive to general changes of opinion, must be resistant to 'lobbies' – that is to say, organized sectional pressures.

Second, freedom of association for industrial purposes raises the issue of wage determination. Under conditions of full employment, can a rising spiral of wages and prices be prevented if collective bargaining, with the right to strike, remains absolutely free? Can the right to strike be limited generally in a free society in peacetime?

Third, freedom in choice of occupations makes it harder to ensure that all men at all times are occupied productively. It makes it impossible to retain men forcibly in particular work or to direct them to it with the threat of imprisonment if they refuse to go. One assumption underlying this Report is that neither the Essential Work Order[9] nor the powers of industrial direction which have been found necessary in war should be continued when the war is over. In Britain at peace the supply of labour cannot be adjusted by decree to the demand for labour; it can only be guided by economic motives. From another angle, freedom in choice of occupation raises also the issue of industrial discipline. Under conditions of full employment, if men are free to move from one employment to another and do not fear dismissal, may not some of them at least become so irregular and undisciplined in their behaviour, as to lower appreciably the efficiency of industry?

Fourth, freedom in the management of a personal income complicates the problem of full employment from another side. If men cannot be forced to buy just what has been produced, this means that the demands for labour and its products cannot be fitted forcibly to the supply. There may be continual changes in the kinds of things on which consumers want to spend their money, that is to say, in the quality of consumers' outlay. There may be changes also in its quantity. For freedom in the management of a personal income includes freedom to decide between spending now and saving so as to have the power of spending later. A totalitarian regime, even if it used money and price and wage differentials to stimulate and guide individual activity, might abolish freedom of saving. It might retain from the national income of each year that portion which it needed for investment, i.e. for the sustenance of persons engaged in making instruments and materials of further production, and might issue to consumers money which, like ration coupons, could not be saved for spending later. In a free society individuals must be allowed to plan their spending over their lives as a whole . . .

None of these freedoms can be exercised irresponsibly. Perpetual instability of economic or social policy would make full employment and any other social reforms futile or impossible. Bargaining for wages must be responsible, looking not to the snatching of short sectional advantages, but to the permanent good of the community. Choice of occupation means freedom in choosing between occupations which are available; it is not possible for an individual to choose to be an Archbishop of Canterbury, if that post is already filled by another. Work means doing what is wanted, not doing just what pleases one. All liberties carry their responsibilities. They must be retained.

In all the respects named, and possibly in some others, the problem of maintaining full employment is more complicated in a free society than it would be under a totalitarian regime. From one complication of some historical importance the problem, as posed here, is free. The list of essential liberties given above does not include liberty of a private citizen to own means of production and to employ other citizens in operating them at a wage. Whether private ownership of means of production to be operated by others is a good economic device or not, it must be judged as a device. It is not an essential citizen liberty in Britain, because it is not and never has been enjoyed by more than a very small proportion of the British people. It cannot even be suggested that any considerable proportion of the people have any lively hope of gaining such ownership later.

On the view taken in this Report, full employment is in fact attainable while leaving the conduct of industry in the main to private enterprise, and the proposals made in the Report are based on this view. But if, contrary to this view, it should be shown by experience or by argument that abolition of private property in the means of production was necessary for full employment, this abolition would have to be undertaken.

1C 'Socialization of Demand' or the Politics of Demand Management

Source: *Full Employment in a Free Society* (1944), pp. 24–5, 205–7.

The meaning and purpose of full employment and the limiting conditions under which it is aimed at in this Report have now been stated. The methods to be adopted depend on diagnosis of the evil to be cured. The Report on Social Insurance and Allied Services began with a diagnosis of Want. The present Report takes as its starting-point a diagnosis of unemployment. The broad results of this diagnosis are as follows.

The volume of unemployment at any time in any community depends upon factors of three kinds: on the factors determining the quantity of the effective demand for the products of industry; on the factors determining the direction of the demand; and on the factors determining the manner in which industry responds to the demand. There will be unemployment if effective demand is not sufficient in total to require use of the whole labour force of the community. There will be unemployment if effective demand, though adequate in total, is misdirected, that is to say, is demand for work of a kind which cannot reasonably be performed by the available labour, or in a place to which the available workmen cannot reasonably be expected to move. There will be unemployment if industry is so organized, that in meeting effective demand it carries excessive reserves of labour standing by to meet local and individual variations of demand, or if there are obstacles which prevent labour from following changes in demand.

In Britain, throughout the period between the two wars, the demand for labour was seriously deficient in total in relation to the supply. Large parts of the country experienced chronic mass unemployment. No part of the country had demand for labour exceeding the supply except possibly for particular classes of labour for a few months at the top of each cyclical fluctuation. In 1937, which was the top of a cyclical fluctuation, representing therefore the best that the unplanned market economy could do, there were in Britain 1.75 million unemployed, more than 10 per cent of the labour force. There were not in the busiest month of 1937 more than a few thousand unfilled vacancies at the employment exchanges, that is to say there were always many times as many unemployed men as vacant jobs. In most of the other years between the wars unemployment was much greater than in 1937.

The demand for labour was not merely inadequate but misdirected. If the demand as a whole had been so much greater quantitatively as to equal the supply as a whole, but had been directed locally in the same way, that is to say, preserving the same proportions between the different regions of Britain, this demand would have failed to abolish unemployment; there would have been large numbers of unfilled vacancies and of men who could not or would not move to fill them, and could not reasonably be required to do so.

Can a policy of full employment be carried through and yield its full benefits under a system in which production is controlled in the main by private enterprise? The policy, as it has been set out here, is primarily one of socializing demand rather than production. It may be found convenient, as a subsidiary measure, to transfer particular industries from private to public ownership, in order to increase the power of the State directly to stabilize demand in a specified sector and in order to bring monopolies under assured control. It will certainly be necessary for the State, by inspection and supervision, to protect the community against risk of exploitation by monopolies and trade associations, in all industries. And it will be necessary for the State, in planning its own outlay, to have full continuous information as to the outlay plans of all large undertakings and to have some power of modifying those plans. But all this is far short of the nationalization of production generally. In particular it leaves the small, independent enterprise, in factory or shop or farm, unaffected. The 'little man' can respond to demand under full employment, as under other conditions. So long as he remains little, he remains subject to competition and the interests of consumers need no further official safeguards.

The policy set out here is one which might be adopted by a community which held firmly to private enterprise, and accepted the principle laid down by an American economist: 'Private industry can and will do the job of production. It is the responsibility of the Government to do its part to ensure a constant demand.' Full employment is achieved in war by State control of demand without socialization of production. There is every reason for hoping that full employment could be secured in peace by the policy outlined here, while leaving the major part of industry to private enterprise. Apart from the problems of international trade, discussed in Part VI; the only significant doubt that arises on this is as to the possibility under such conditions, of bringing about a sufficient stability of private investment, and preventing its cyclical fluctuations. It is reasonable to let that doubt be resolved by experience.

It can be argued, nevertheless, that under such conditions a policy of full employment, even if it gave full employment, would fail to yield its full benefits and might lead to dangerous consequences. It can be urged that all that is proposed here is insufficient, without the socialization of production in all its more important forms. This position may be supported by a variety of arguments. In the first place, as has been pointed out above, the smooth working of a full employment policy involves the co-operation of workpeople, in enforcing industrial discipline on the unruly, in securing maximum efficiency and removal of restrictions on output, in refraining from pressing unreasonable claims that might set up a vicious spiral of wages and prices. Can that co-operation, it is asked, be secured under conditions of enterprise conducted for private profit? It is argued, in the second place, that a State policy of full employment will always be liable to sabotage by capitalists desiring to make difficulties for the State. It is argued, in the third place, that substitution of national for private ownership of the means of production is necessary to prevent the piling up of wealth which may be used to manipulate the political machine. It is argued, finally, that full employment will not by itself bring about the more equal distribution of income which is essential to social justice.

These arguments raise large issues, economic, political and moral, which fall to a large extent outside the scope of this Report. The importance of these issues is obvious. They are not prejudged in what is written here. The proposals of this Report are designed for one essential practical purpose – to bring to an end the mass unemployment and the fear of unemployment which, next to war, have been the greatest evils of modern times. The proposals take us round the next corner ahead – a corner which must be turned, if we desire to preserve free institutions. The problems that lie beyond that corner will become clearer when that corner has been passed; they can, if we so desire, be left to be dealt with when they are reached.

The basic proposals of this Report are neither socialism nor an alternative to socialism: they are required and will work under capitalism and under socialism alike, and whether the sector of industry conducted by private enterprise is large or is small. A conscious control of the economic system at the highest level – a new type of budget which takes manpower as its datum – adequate sustained directed demand for the products of industry – organization of the labour market – these are required in any modern society. These things the State must provide in any case, if the citizens want full employment. What else the State may be called on to do has to be determined on other grounds, or can at need be decided later. From the point of view of full employment, the decision depends largely on how private citizens use their liberties. If trade unions under full employment press wage claims unreasonably, maintenance of a stable price level will become impossible; wage determination will perforce become a function of the State. If the private owners of business undertakings under full employment set out to exploit consumers by organizing monopolies and price rings, or abuse their economic power for political purposes, or fail, with all the help of the State and in an expanding economy, to stabilize the process of investment, the private owners cannot for long be left in their ownership. If the people of Britain generally under full employment become undisciplined in industry, that will show either that they are not sufficiently civilized to be led by anything but fear of unemployment and are unworthy of freedom, or that the control of industry must be changed. All liberties have their responsibilities. The greater the sense of citizen responsibility, the greater can be the measure of liberty and the scope that is left for agencies independent of the State.

1D 'Assumptions, Methods and Principles' in the 1942 Social Insurance Plan

Source: SIAS (1942), pp. 120–2

Scope of Social Security:

The term 'social security' is used here to denote the securing of an income to take the place of earnings when they are interrupted by unemployment, sickness or accident, to provide for retirement through age, to provide against loss of support by the death of another person, and to meet exceptional expenditures, such as those connected with birth, death and marriage. Primarily social security means security of income up to a minimum, but the provision of an income should be associated with treatment designed to bring the interruption of earnings to an end as soon as possible.

Three Assumptions:

No satisfactory scheme of social security can be devised except on the following assumptions:—

(A) children's allowances for children up to the age of 15 or if in full-time education up to the age of 16;
(B) comprehensive health and rehabilitation services for prevention and cure of disease and restoration of capacity for work, available to all members of the community;
(C) maintenance of employment, that is to say avoidance of mass unemployment.

The grounds for making these three assumptions, the methods of satisfying them and their relation to the social security scheme are discussed later. Children's allowances will be added to all the insurance benefits and pensions described below.

Three Methods of Security:

On these three assumptions, a Plan for Social Security is outlined below, combining three distinct methods: social insurance for basic needs: national assistance for special cases; voluntary insurance for additions to the basic provision. Social insurance means the providing of cash payments conditional upon compulsory contributions previously made by, or on behalf of, the insured persons, irrespective of the resources of the individual at the time of the claim. Social insurance is much the most important of the three methods and is proposed here in a form as comprehesive as possible. But while social insurance can, and should, be the main instrument for guaranteeing income security, it cannot be the only one. It needs to be supplemented both by national assistance and by voluntary insurance. National assistance means the giving of cash payments conditional upon proved need at the time of the claim, irrespective of previous contributions but adjusted by consideration of individual circumstances and paid from the national exchequer. Assistance is an indispensable supplement to social insurance, however the scope of the latter may be widened. In addition to both of these there is place for voluntary insurance. Social insurance and national assistance organized by the State are designed to guarantee, on condition of service, a basic income for subsistence. The actual incomes and by consequence the normal standards of expenditure of different sections of the population differ greatly. Making provision for these higher standards is primarily the function of the individual, that is to say, it is a matter for free choice and voluntary insurance. But the State should make sure that its measures leave room and encouragement for such voluntary insurance. The social insurance scheme is the greater part of the Plan for Social Security and its description occupies most of this Part of the Report. But the plan includes national assistance and voluntary insurance as well.

Six Principles of Social Insurance:

The social insurance scheme set out below as the chief method of social security embodies six fundamental principles:

Flat rate of subsistence benefit
Flat rate of contribution
Unification of administrative responsibility
Adequacy of benefit
Comprehensiveness
Classification

Flat Rate of Subsistence Benefit:

The first fundamental principle of the social insurance scheme is provision of a flat rate of insurance benefit, irrespective of the amount of the earnings which have been interrupted by unemployment or disability or ended by retirement; exception is made only where prolonged disability has resulted from an industrial accident or disease. This principle follows from the recognition of the place and importance of voluntary insurance in social security and distinguishes the scheme proposed for Britain from the security schemes of Germany, the Soviet Union, the United States and most other countries with the exception of New Zealand. The flat rate is the same for all the principal forms of cessation of earning – unemployment, disability, retirement; for maternity and for widowhood there is a temporary benefit at a higher rate.

Flat Rate of Contribution:

The second fundamental principle of the scheme is that the compulsory contribution required of each insured person or his employer is at a flat rate, irrespective of his means. All insured persons, rich or poor, will pay the same contributions for the same security; those with larger means will pay more only to the extent that as taxpayers they pay more to the National Exchequer and so to the State share of the Social Insurance Fund. This feature distinguishes the scheme proposed for Britain from the scheme recently established in New Zealand under which the contributions are graduated by income, and are in effect an income tax assigned to a particular service. Subject moreover to one exception, the contribution will be the same irrespective of the assumed degree of risk affecting particular individuals or forms of employment. The exception is the raising of a proportion of the special cost of benefits and pensions for industrial disability in occupations of high risk by a levy on employers proportionate to risk and payroll.

Unification of Administrative Responsibility:

The third fundamental principle is unification of administrative responsibility in the interests of efficiency and economy. For each insured person there will be a single weekly contribution, in respect of all his benefits. There will be in each locality a security office able to deal with claims of every kind and all sides of security. The methods of paying different kinds of cash benefit will be different and will take account of the circumstances of insured persons, providing for payment at the home or elsewhere, as is necessary. All contributions will be paid into a single Social Insurance Fund and all benefits and other insurance payments will be paid from that fund.

Adequacy of Benefit:

The fourth fundamental principle is adequacy of benefit in amount and in time. The flat rate of benefit proposed is intended in itself to be sufficient without further resources to provide the minimum income needed for subsistence in all normal cases. It gives room and a basis for additional voluntary provision, but does not assume that in any case. The benefits are adequate also in time, that is to say, except for contingencies of a temporary nature, they will continue indefinitely without means test, so long as the need continues, though subject to any change of conditions and treatment required by prolongation of the interruption in earning and occupation.

Comprehensiveness:

The fifth fundamental principle is that social insurance should be comprehensive, in respect both of the persons covered and of their needs. It should not leave either to national assistance or to voluntary insurance any risk so general or so uniform that social insurance can be justified. For national assistance involves a means test which may discourage voluntary insurance or personal saving. And voluntary insurance can never be sure of covering the ground. For any need moreover which, like direct funeral expenses, is so general and so uniform as to be a fit subject for insurance by compulsion, social insurance is much cheaper to administer than voluntary insurance.

Classification:

The sixth fundamental principle is that social insurance, while unified and comprehensive, must take account of the different way of life of different sections of the community; of those dependent on earnings by employment under contract of service, of those earning in other ways, of those rendering vital unpaid service as housewives, of those not yet of age to earn and of those past earning. The term 'classification' is used here to denote adjustment of insurance to the differing circumstances of each of these classes and to many varieties of need and circumstance within each insurance class. But the insurance classes are not economic or social classes in the ordinary sense; the insurance scheme is one for all citizens irrespective of their means.

1E   The Case for Voluntary Action

Source: Voluntary Action (1948), pp. 318–23

The State should encourage Voluntary Action of all kinds for social advance . . . It should in every field of its growing activity use where it can, without destroying their freedom and their spirit, the voluntary agencies for social advance, born of social conscience and of philanthropy. This is one of the marks of a free society.

The *Report on Social Insurance and Allied Services*, submitted by me to the Government in November, 1942, set out a practical programme for putting first things first. There was to be bread and health for all at all times before cake and circuses for anybody at any time, so far as this order of priority could be enforced by redistribution of money. The plan for social security put forward in my first Report was in essence a plan for redistributing money, as between times of earning and not earning, as between richer and poorer. It took money from people when they had money, took money in the form of social insurance contributions and general taxation, in order to hand back to people, when they could not earn, enough money to buy the necessities of healthy life, and in order to pay for medical treatment of all kinds when they needed treatment.

This first Report was not put forward as anything but a first step. Bread and health are not all that a citizen needs. Idleness even with bread demoralizes. I followed the first Report as soon as possible by a second Report in October, 1944, suggesting how Full Employment in a Free Society could be achieved. The second Report was unlike the first Report in being unofficial, not made at the request of the Government. It was like the first Report in being largely, though not wholly, concerned with the management of money. It emphasized the fact that the State is or can be master of money, while in a money economy all individuals are controlled by money. The State alone can ensure that at all times unsatisfied needs are clothed with purchasing power, so as to turn them into effective demand goods and services. The State alone, by its management of money, can prevent there being at one and the same time in a community unsatisfied needs, and idle men and machinery by whose employment those needs could be met. The programme for full employment in a free society was expressed as in essence a programme for socializing demand rather than socializing production. The State was to do that which the State alone can do: manage money so as to maintain spending. Subject to that, the State should leave as much as possible to the initiative and enterprise of the citizens.

The sting of this third Report, on Voluntary Action, lies in showing that the aim of the first Report, of putting first things first, cannot be accomplished simply by redistribution of purchasing power. Money, however well distributed, will not buy the material necessaries of healthy life for all, if they are not being produced in sufficient quantities for all. There are some things – not goods but services – which often cannot be bought with money, but may be rendered from sense of duty. Clearly in Britain today first things are not in practice being put first. It is not putting first things first to rank an idle Saturday before decent homes for all; to let scarce manpower go to build cinemas or holiday camps while old people struggle in solitude with discomforts beyond their strength, while sick men suffer needlessly for want of hospitals, while handicapped adults who have learned a trade cannot use it because they find no place to live, while handicapped children miss the training that might make them useful citizens, while for many thousands of married pairs life in their own homes remains impossible and unnatural living makes unhappy families.

If we ask why, with complete democratic control of our Government, with social security established by law and full employment established in practice, life in Britain is not better than we find it today, the answer is twofold.

First, the State is or can be master of money, but in a free society it is master of very little else. The making of a good society depends not on the State but on the citizens, acting individually or in free association with one another, acting on motives of various kinds, some selfish, others unselfish, some narrow and material, others inspired by love of man and love of God. The happiness or unhappiness of the society in which we live depends upon ourselves as citizens, not on the instrument of political power which we call the State.

Second, we citizens of Britain have been slow to recognize how in fifty years with two world wars the world around us has changed, and calls for a change in our behaviour. We have not realized sufficiently how much of our easy prosperity in the nineteenth century we owed to the accident of being the first nation to become industrial . . . Prosperity will no longer come to us as easily as in the past. If we want to live as well as our fathers, we must either work harder or work more effectively, not rejecting or limiting any machine that will make work easier, nor rejecting or obstructing the utmost use of manpower in any form.

This third Report is not concerned with the immediate task of making our people prosperous again, able to help themselves and to help others. But it is designed to show some of the tasks that must be undertaken if prosperity when it comes is to mean the chance of happiness for all. This Report shows . . . how much unhappiness remains in Britain, untouched by social security and full employment. That is the negative side of the Report. The positive side is more important . . . The positive side of this third Report is in the earlier chapters which show how much the making of better conditions of life has owed to Voluntary Action. The world at large is engaged in debating, sometimes by reason and voting, sometimes in other ways, the advantages and disadvantages of private enterprise in business. This third Report is concerned with private enterprise, not in business but in the service of mankind, not for gain but under the driving power of social conscience. The need for private enterprise in that form is beyond debate.

If we are really to put first things first, bread and health for all at all times before cake and circuses for anybody, we must go beyond the simple redistribution of money to the much harder task of ensuring production of goods and services, to provision not in money but in kind. We must continue to use to the full the spirit that made our great organizations for Mutual Aid and that fired the philanthropists of the past. It is necessary to face two new difficulties in the way of doing this.

First, it involves making and keeping something other than pursuit of gain as the dominant force in society. The business motive, in the field covered by this Report, is seen in continual or repeated conflict with the philanthropic motive, and has too often been successful. The industrial assurance offices exploited successfully for gain a universal desire to avoid a pauper burial. They have been succeeded by the businesses of football pools, dog tracks and cinemas, all exploiting in different ways for personal gain the increased leisure of the people. The business motive is a good servant but a bad master, and a society which gives itself up to the dominance of the business motive is a bad society. We do not put first things first in putting ourselves first. In former days there was a great alternative to the pursuit of gain, as the guiding force in society; there was force for good inspired by religious belief and based on membership of a Christian community. Now this religious force for good is less widely influential than it was in the nineteenth century. It must either be revived or be replaced by some equally good alternative, if that can be found. Perhaps it must be both in part revived and in part replaced.

Second, with the passage from class rule to representative democracy, little can be done except by influencing directly, not a few leaders, but the mass of the people. We shall not take the difficult steps of going beyond redistribution of money to provision in kind, unless we really want to do this, and 'we' for this purpose means in Britain now the whole people – the democracy. In the unequal society of the past there were always dynamic individuals with social conscience, and, in giving their personal service, they could usually get the necessary help for their purposes from the superfluities of money and leisure among their friends. In the society of the future there will still be dynamic individuals with consciences, but they may not so easily find the material means of doing their work, and they will not find it in the same way. Democracy today has to show that in discarding the inequalities it can learn the virtues of aristocracy.

2

Social Insurance and the Allied Services: the Political Utopia of 1942

The ambition of *SIAS* should not be denigrated and the importance of this 1942 report should not be underestimated. The report proposed a comprehensive range of social security benefits which were to be substantially more generous than those which had been paid before the Second World War (extract 2B). If that ambition was never realized (Chapter 3, extract 3E), *SIAS* did define the shape of the public welfare system for more than a generation after 1945. But, when the postwar social security system never worked as Beveridge had intended in 1942, *SIAS* must be evaluated critically. It cannot be assumed that all our problems with social security can be attributed to successive governments which failed to implement and sustain the proposals of 1942. The conclusion of our criticism is that the 1942 report was politically utopian; Beveridge's commitment to the *a priori* of liberal collectivism led him to propose an ideal scheme for social improvement which was impracticable in that it was incapable of realization.

Ideologically motivated schemes for welfare reform typically work through constructing an object or a problem and then specifying politically congenial instruments which will resolve the difficulty. Thus, the Benthamite 1834 Royal Commission on the Poor Laws took as its object the hedonism of the labourer which manifested itself in a problem of pauperism under the old poor law. The moral character of the labourers was, on this view, being undermined by the availability of poor law relief: honest labourers slipped from being poor but industrious to being paupers maintained by public subventions. The solution was to apply the principle of 'less eligibility' through the administrative instrument of the 'well-regulated workhouse' which would make relief less attractive than independence. Beveridge's liberal collectivist report of 1942 worked in the same way. It took as its object the problem of primary poverty which Beveridge called 'want'. The aim of the social security system was to eliminate such poverty. For Beveridge compulsory social insurance was the privileged instrument for alleviating poverty; insurance was to be expanded to dominate the field of income maintenance where it would support 'all normal cases' (extract 2D). The broad strategy of the 1942 report has already been summarized in extract 1D in the previous chapter. The extracts in this chapter show how the political *a priori* entered into Beveridge's construction of the social problem and led to the policy recommendation of social insurance.

If we are concerned with the construction of the object of poverty or 'want' then we must consider Beveridge's relation to poverty surveys. This type of social investigation developed from Rowntree's first York survey[1] which introduced the concept of 'primary poverty' to describe the plight of those who had insufficient income to maintain 'physical efficiency' even if they disposed of their income rationally on strictly subsistence necessities. In the 1942 report Beveridge relied on the concepts, procedures and results of the interwar poverty surveys which he represented as the factual or 'impartial scientific' basis for his analysis of the social problem.

> The plan is based on a diagnosis of want. It starts from facts, from the condition of the people as revealed by social surveys between the wars. (*SIAS*, 1942, p. 8)

To begin with, Beveridge argued that the surveys showed that the main cause of want was 'interruption of earnings' and most of the rest was attributable to large family size (extract 2A). Comprehensive social insurance was to be applied to bridging the gaps in earnings disclosed by the poverty surveys. More fundamentally, Beveridge borrowed the object of 'poverty' and the operational procedures for measuring the income necessary for subsistence through adding up necessary expenditure on food, rent, clothing, fuel and other items. A subcommittee of poverty survey investigators was employed to advise Beveridge on the calculation of a subsistence minimum (extract 2C). In the poverty surveys this calculation defined a poverty line below which households lacked the minimum necessary income; in *SIAS* the calculation specified a target for redirecting the state income maintenance system which would provide income support up to this minimum.

The notion of poverty is still used polemically by the left. It is therefore worth insisting that the concepts and procedures of the poverty survey do not have an inherently 'progressive' character; as we have argued elsewhere (Williams, 1981) they were used before the First World War to argue the case for free trade and temperance. But in Beveridge's work of the 1940s, the poverty surveys are used to vindicate the political problematic of liberal collectivism in dealing with social issues.

The object of poverty was intially crucial because it demarcated a limited sphere of state action; it focused attention on the issue of a deficiency of income at the bottom end of the range of distribution and it diverted attention from the issue of inequality and the whole distribution of income from top to bottom. With the object of poverty established, Beveridge was able to use the findings of the surveys to sustain a series of classic liberal collectivist positions on the distribution of income. Poverty represented a problem of maldistribution of income which had not been rectified on the free market through the mechanism of rising real incomes; the surveys showed that real wages had increased by one-third since 1900 and yet this had not 'reduce[d] want to insignificance' (extract 2B). At the same time poverty set up a distributional problem which could be rectified without upsetting the whole range of income inequalities. Indeed interclass redistribution between 'land, capital, management and labour' would be diversionary. Intraclass redistribution was 'required among wage-earners themselves, as between times of earning and not earning, and between times of heavy family responsibilities and of light or no family responsibilities' (extract 2B). Beveridge quite explicitly stopped short of recommending that redistribution should be confined to the working class but he could not resist making the point that redistribution could be confined to the working class. The surveys showed that the income surplus of working-class families above the poverty line was very much larger than the income deficit of those below the poverty line and the implication was that 'want could have been abolished before the present war by a redistribution of income within the wage-earning classes' (extract 2B).

When promoting his social security scheme, Beveridge often described it as part 'of a policy of a national minimum' (e.g. extract 2E, or *Pillars of Security*, 1943, p. 143). The reference to the slogan of the Webbs' 1909 Royal Commission Minority Report[2] was no doubt deliberate. But the implied suggestion of continuity was unjustified because problem definitions and policy recommendations shifted dramatically between 1909 and 1942. For the Webbs the social reformer's task was to discriminate the heterogeneous problems presented by different kinds of unemployment, sickness and old age; the group of the unemployed, for example, included four distinct kinds of unemployed person including underemployed casuals and unemployables. The policy recommendation of 1909 was for 'curative and restorative treatment' which entailed large-scale provision of services with relief and assistance made conditional upon behaviour. The Webbs' design of 1909 would have imposed a comprehensive system of tutelage upon the working class. Beveridge's strategy of 1942 was very different. When the object of poverty was dominant, *SIAS* did not emphasize the heterogeneity of social problems; in this framework all problems were reduced to the common denominator of insufficient income and the task of social security was to rectify this deficiency through redistribution. The policy recommendation of 1942 was for more and better insurance cash benefits, paid as of right by virtue of contribution; behavioural conditions would be imposed only on a minority of long-term cases (extract 2F). The Beveridge design of 1942 proposed to extend and generalize a contractual relation between the individual insurance contributor and the state.

At this time the technique of contributory insurance had a fiscal advantage over non-contributory assistance. After its late-nineteenth-century introduction in Germany, the innovative technique of social insurance spread rapidly because it helped solve the problem of paying for social reform. As Beveridge recognized, insurance represented a way of recovering 'a substantial part of the cost of benefits as contributions' (*SIAS*, 1942, p. 12). In the scheme he proposed, employer and employee contributions covered 48 per cent of the total cost in 1948 and 38 per cent of the cost in 1965 (*SIAS*, 1942, p. 112). Any alternative assistance scheme would have had to be financed out of increased general taxation. This was technically problematic in 1942 when the PAYE system (for cumulative withholding of tax out of current income) was a wartime innovation and it was not clear whether the working classes would pay income tax after the war was over. The kind of social insurance which Beveridge proposed was very different from private insurance; the Beveridge scheme was unfunded, there was no actuarial relation between contributions and benefits and no attempt to adjust premium for individual risk. Keynes concluded that the whole notion of social insurance was an empty fiction which concealed a convenient form of taxation. Beveridge's position was different because he believed that the form of insurance had an inherent political virtue.

For Beveridge, the state's response to poverty should not take the form of a philanthropy which offered gifts (in the form of means-tested assistance allowances) to the needy. Beveridge believed that means tests discouraged 'the duty and pleasure of thrift' (extract 2D) and thus diminished private saving and voluntary insurance which were necessary for liberal collectivism if the sphere of social independence was to be as large as possible (*SIAS*, 1942, p. 51). More positively, in the framework of liberal collectivism, the form of social insurance was in itself valuable because it established the relation between the citizen and the state on a new contractual basis. With insurance generalized, the state's response to poverty would take the form of a conditional exchange where both partners had mutual rights and responsibilities. The state would be relieved of some of the cost of social security and would at the same time accept the new and higher 'responsibility of seeing that unemployment and disease are reduced to the minimum' (extract 2D). Citizens would gain the right to unconditional maintenance by virtue of contribution and would at the same time accept a responsibility for not drawing benefit unnecessarily. In this context, the political advantage of social insurance was that it had a public educative function. The possibility of demoralized dependence was reduced by social insurance because the individual as contributor acquired an interest in economical adminstration. Beveridge saw social insurance as a kind of politico-moral theatre whose representations would lead the working class into the ways of independence.

> The citizens as insured persons should realize that they cannot get more than certain benefits for certain contributions, should have a motive to support measures for economical administration, should not be taught to regard the State as the dispenser of gifts for which no one needs to pay. (*SIAS*, 1942, p. 100)

This liberal collectivist solicitude for promoting independence through state maintenance emerges even more clearly if we examine the particular form of social insurance which Beveridge's report recommended. Social insurance is not a single technique but a field of choice of techniques. The cost of this kind of welfare can be variably apportioned between employers, employees and the state while the redistributive effects can be further adjusted by the choice of flat rate or graduated benefits and contributions. One of the most important, and most neglected, sections of the Beveridge Report is Appendix F on 'comparisons with other countries' (extract 2E). This shows that Beveridge's choice of flat rate contributions and benefits was an unusual one. Although the British had favoured flat rate contributions and benefits since 1911, graduated earnings-related social insurance schemes were the norm in other countries. Only Eire, which had inherited the British system, operated a flat rate system while New Zealand had graduated tax contributions for flat rate benefits. Beveridge's reasons for preferring a flat rate system always included (e.g. extract 2E), and sometimes solely consisted of, a liberal collectivist justification:

> to give by compulsory insurance more than is needed for subsistence is an unnecessary interference with individual responsibilities. More can be given only by taking more in contributions or taxation. That means departing from the principle of a national minimum, above which citizens shall spend their money freely, and adopting instead the principle of regulating the lives of individuals by law. (*SIAS*, 1942, p. 118)

The argument so far shows how the liberal collectivist *a priori* figures in both the overall problem definition and the general policy recommendations of 1942. *SIAS* is an intellectual tour de force because Beveridge develops and sustains his political position with remorseless logicality in the treatment of detail. As we have argued elsewhere (Cutler *et al.*, 1986), the maximizing of personal responsibility and the maintenance of the preconditions for social independence are the dominant considerations in Beveridge's treatment of detail such as entitlement to family allowances, differentiation of long- and short-term benefit rates and uniformity of benefit in sickness and unemployment.

If the report of 1942 has a high degree of internal coherence, it is also true that the report could not easily be implemented. There were two fundamental problems here. First, the objective of eliminating poverty was not a straightforward one. Second, Beveridge's chosen instrument was inadequate to the task because social insurance could not easily cover the whole field of income maintenance. These two points can be considered in turn.

The objective of eliminating poverty could not be straightforward when it was practically impossible to measure subsistence poverty. The subtotals of necessary expenditure on food, rent, clothing and so forth could all be disputed. When house rents varied within and between different regions, Beveridge's subcommittee of poverty experts was unable to agree on an allowance figure for rent. Beveridge finally chose an allowance figure of 10 shillings (50p) per week which was just below the national average payment for rent. But this was arbitrary when a majority of households paid rents which were 2 shillings and 6 pence (12p) more or less than the allowance (extract 2C). The subcommittee's estimates for necessary expenditure on food were no more secure. The estimates here depended on the construction of a dietary which represented a cultural pattern of consumption rather than a subsistence minimum. The League of Nations and British Medical Association dietaries used in *SIAS* included meat although vegetarianism was a more economical alternative for the working class. In other areas the concessions to culture were more half-hearted. Every couple was allocated an allowance of 2 shillings (10p) per week to cover inefficient purchasing and diversion of expenditure on to non-essentials; the average working-class family in the 1930s spent 7 shillings (35p) per week on drink alone. As an attempt to specify a minimum necessary income, the *SIAS* calculation was completely unsatisfactory. Its procedures were so much pseudo-science which provided a convenient support for liberal collectivism which misrepresented them as a scientific point of departure.

The impossibility of measuring poverty might not have mattered if insurance could have been extended so that it paid more generous allowances to all claimants of state income maintenance. Whatever assumptions were made about the postwar social problem, it was always unlikely that the cover provided by insurance (available as a right) would be sufficient to reduce to insignificance the need to fall back on to assistance (available only after a means test). The problems here were covered up by Beveridge's repeated insistence that the problem was one of 'interruption or loss of earning power' (e.g.

SIAS, 1942, p. 7). Beveridge did not discriminate between short- and long-term dependence or discuss how the balance between the two kinds of dependence would shift as and when the number of old people increased and the number of unemployed varied. If full employment was maintained, as it was through the 1950s and 1960s, the dependence problem would inevitably centre on chronic sickness and on retirement which could involve an interruption of earning power of ten years or more at the end of a working life. It was simply very difficult in the short term to extend a contributory insurance scheme to cover retirement. In 1942 Beveridge proposed a 20-year lead-in to the payment of full subsistence pensions; those who retired before 1965 would be paid a lower pension which would be scaled according to contribution record. As the next chapter shows (extract 3E), the coalition government rejected the rising scale in favour of a flat rate standard pension which would be paid regardless of contribution at a rate which was substantially below that which Beveridge had envisaged. Either way, assistance would clearly play a major role in topping up inadequate insurance allowances.

If mass unemployment returned, that complicated matters further. As Beveridge recognized, '*no* scheme of social insurance is satisfactory if there is mass unemployment' (*Pillars of Security*, 1943, p. 139). The finances of social insurance could be adjusted to cope with quite high rates of unemployment; Beveridge's provisional social security budget was costed on the prudently pessimistic basis of a 10 per cent general rate of unemployment (extract 2F). The crucial point was that whatever the level of unemployment, old age pensions would be the major drain on the insurance fund; on Beveridge's projections unemployment insurance benefit would account for only one-fifth of social insurance expenditure and one-eighth of the whole social security budget (*SIAS*, 1942, p. 104). On this basis it was possible to construct an insurance scheme whose fund would balance at unemployment levels of 10 per cent or more. But Beveridge himself conceded that unemployment insurance would be inappropriate in these circumstances. A cash benefit was not in itself enough for the long-term unemployed; those who drew unemployment benefit for more than 26 weeks would be obliged to attend a training centre (extract 2F). It was recognized that this proposal was impractical 'if it has to be applied to men by the million or the hundred thousand' (extract 2F). But at the same time Beveridge implausibly supposed that this would not be a problem because long-term unemployment of the same individual for more than 26 weeks 'would be reduced to a negligible amount' (*SIAS*, 1942, p. 185). Given a heterogeneous working population which contained some unemployment-prone individuals, long unemployment could only be curbed by constant over-full employment.

When the problem was 'interruption of earnings', it was impossible to avoid the issue of how and to what extent earnings would be interrupted. But this problem definition served to conceal some subtler assumptions. In effect the Beveridge plan assumed two-parent households with the wife engaged in the 'vital but unpaid labour' of child-rearing while the husband held a full-time job at standard wages adequate to maintain a couple and at least one child. This last assumption was never made explicit but it was implicit in the design of the proposed social security system which concentrated insurance and assistance benefits on the unwaged. Wage subvention had a very limited role; Beveridge's major proposal here was for child allowances on the second and subsequent children. In the context of the 1930s, when no more than 1 in 7 of married women worked and marriages lasted, this may have been reasonable. It was anachronistic by the mid-1980s when half of married women worked and there were more than a million single parents. Of course, it is pointless to criticize Beveridge for failing to foresee the future. But it should be noted that the Beveridge plan depended as much on assumptions about the composition of available employment as it did on assumptions about the level of unemployment. By the mid-1970s the tragedy was that the level of unemployment was increasing at the same time as the composition of employment was deteriorating; in the past thirty years we have lost more than 3 million relatively well-paid, full-time jobs for semi or unskilled male factory workers. The kind of secondary income maintenance which Beveridge proposed can only succeed where primary income distribution through the wages system is satisfactory and that primary result has become increasingly problematic in the period since the long boom collapsed in the mid-1970s.

Twenty years before this, it was already clear that the Beveridge scheme of social insurance had major defects. The fundamental problem was that Beveridge willed the end of generous income maintenance but for political reasons he could only contemplate the means of flat rate insurance which was not adequate to achieving this

51

end. He claimed that 'the finance of the social insurance scheme is not rigid: it is elastic' (*Pillars of Security*, 1943, p. 143). But Beveridge's own proposals for finance effectively admitted that flat rate social insurance did not have an adequate revenue base; the insurance fund had to be relieved of all the cost of child allowances and under the 20-year lead-in provision the fund was also relieved of part of the cost of maintaining old age pensioners. Flat rate contributions put a severe constraint on the scale or scope of benefits. Beveridge correctly identified the employer's contribution as a 'tax on employment' and the employee's contribution as a regressive 'poll tax' (*SIAS*, 1942, p. 109). Since the flat rate contributions were regressive, there was a limit to how far they could be pushed; given a limit on the exchequer contributions to the insurance fund, flat rate contributions meant severe restrictions on benefit levels and/or coverage. This inevitably meant that the role of assistance would (one way or another) turn out to be larger and more permanent than Beveridge had intended.

The fundamental flaw of the 1942 Beveridge Report was that the design of assistance was subordinated to the requirements of an insurance scheme which could not practically cover the whole field of income maintenance. In Beveridge's scheme, there had to be a means test for assistance benefits so as to encourage insurance contributors whose benefits would not be means tested;

> assistance will be available to meet all needs which are not covered by insurance. It must meet those needs adequately up to subsistence level, but it must be felt to be something less desirable than insurance benefit; otherwise the insured persons get nothing for their contributions. Assistance, therefore, will be given subject always to proof of means and on examination of needs. (*SIAS*, 1942, p. 141)

Society would have to suffer the consequences in terms of low take-up because claimants did not know what or how to claim or because claimants were unwilling to claim. Beveridge never intended to create an income maintenance system where means tests were a major feature for he recognized that 'in practice, such a system would not lead to abolition of want, because the citizens would in many cases suffer want rather than submit to investigation of their needs and means' (*Pillars of Security*, 1943, pp. 121–2). But that was the unintended consequence of his unreasonable view that the one politically congenial principle of insurance could cover the whole field of social needs in income maintenance.

2A   The Problem of 'Interruption of Earnings' as Disclosed by the Interwar Poverty Surveys

Source: SIAS (1942), pp. 7–8

The Plan for Social Security . . . starts from a diagnosis of want – of the circumstances in which, in the years preceding the present war, families and individuals in Britain might lack the means of healthy subsistence. During those years impartial scientific authorities made social surveys of the conditions of life in a number of principal towns in Britain, including London, Liverpool, Sheffield, Plymouth, Southampton, York and Bristol. They determined the proportions of the people in each town whose means were below the standard assumed to be necessary for subsistence, and they analysed the extent and causes of that deficiency. From each of these social surveys the same broad result emerges. Of all the want shown by the surveys, from three-quarters to five-sixths, according to the precise standard chosen for want, was due to interruption or loss of earning power. Practically the whole of the remaining one-quarter to one-sixth was due to failure to relate income during earning to the size of the family. These surveys were made before the introduction of supplementary pensions had reduced the amount of poverty amongst old persons. But this does not affect the main conclusion to be drawn from these surveys: abolition of want requires a double redistribution of income, through social insurance and by family needs.

Abolition of want requires, first, improvement of State insurance, that is to say provision against interruption and loss of earning power. All the principal causes of interruption or loss of earnings are now the subject of schemes of social insurance. If, in spite of these schemes, so many persons unemployed or sick or old or widowed are found to be without adequate income for subsistence according to the standards adopted in the social surveys, this means that the benefits amount to less than subsistence by those standards or do not last as long as the need, and that the assistance which supplements insurance is either insufficient in amount or available only on terms which make men unwilling to have recourse to it. None of the insurance benefits provided before the war were in fact designed with reference to the standards of the social surveys. Though unemployment benefit was not altogether out of relation to those standards, sickness and disablement benefit, old age pensions and widows' pensions were far below them, while workmen's compensation was below subsistence level for anyone who had family responsibilities, or whose earnings in work were less than twice the amount needed for subsistence. To prevent interruption or destruction of earning power from leading to want, it is necessary to improve the present schemes of social insurance in three directions: by extension of scope to cover persons now excluded, by extension of purposes to cover risks now excluded, and by raising the rates of benefit.

Abolition of want requires, second, adjustment of incomes, in periods of earning as well as in interruption of earning, to family needs, that is to say, in one form or another it requires allowances for children. Without such allowances as part of benefit or added to it, to make provision for large families, no social insurance against interruption of earnings can be adequate. But, if children's allowances are given only when earnings are interrupted and are not given during earning also, two evils are unavoidable. First, a substantial measure of acute want will remain among the lower paid workers as the accompaniment of large families. Second, in all such cases, income will be greater during unemployment or other interruptions of work than during work.

By a double redistribution of income through social insurance and children's allowances, want, as defined in the social surveys, could have been abolished in Britain before the present war.

2B The Practicability of Redistributing Income so as to Abolish Want

Source: *SIAS* (1942), pp. 165–7

The aim of the Plan for Social Security is to abolish want by ensuring that every citizen willing to serve according to his powers has at all times an income sufficient to meet his responsibilities. Is this aim likely to be within our reach immediately after the present war?

The first step in considering the prospective economic resources of the community after the present war is to see what they were just before the war. The social surveys made by impartial investigators of living conditions in some of the main industrial centres of Britain between 1928 and 1937 have been used earlier in this Report to supply a diagnosis of want. They can be used also to show that the total resources of the community were sufficient to make want needless. While, in every town surveyed, substantial percentages of the families examined had less than the bare minimum for subsistence, the great bulk of them had substantially more than the minimum. In East London, in the week chosen for investigation in 1929, while one family in every nine had income below the minimum and was in want, nearly two-thirds of all the families had at least 20/- [£1] a week more than the minimum, and nearly a third had 40/- [£2] a week more than the minimum; these were actual incomes after allowing for sickness, unemployment and irregular work. In Bristol the average working-class family enjoyed a standard of living more than 100 per cent above its minimum needs; while one Bristol family in nine in the year 1937 was in sheer physical want, two families out of every five had half as much again as they needed for subsistence. Similar contrasts were presented in every survey. Another way of putting these contrasts is to compare the surplus of those who had more than the minimum with the deficiency of those who had less. In East London, the total surplus of the working-class families above the minimum was more than thirty times the total deficiency of those below it. In York, where Mr Rowntree in 1936 used a much higher minimum – the standard of human needs containing more than bare physical necessaries of food, clothing, fuel and housing – the three classes of the working population living above the standard had a total surplus above it at least eight times the total deficiency of the two classes living below the standard. Want could have been abolished before the present war by a redistribution of income within the wage-earning classes, without touching any of the wealthier classes. This is said not to suggest that redistribution of income should be confined to the wage-earning classes; still less is it said to suggest that men should be content with avoidance of want, with subsistence incomes. It is said simply as the most convincing demonstration that abolition of want just before this war was easily within the economic resources of the community; want was a needless scandal due to not taking the trouble to prevent it.

The social surveys showed not only what was the standard of living available to the community just before the war but also that it had risen rapidly in the past thirty or forty years. The recent London and York surveys were designed to provide comparisons with earlier studies. They yielded unquestionable proof of large and general progress. When the New Survey of London Life and Labour was made in 1929, the average workman in London could buy a third more of articles of consumption in return for labour of an hour's less duration per day than he could buy forty years before at the time of Charles Booth's[3] original survey. The standard of living available to the workpeople of York in 1936 may be put overall at about 30 per cent higher than it was in 1899. This improvement of economic conditions was reflected in improvement of physical conditions. In London, the crude death rate fell from 18.6 per thousand in 1900 to 11.4 in 1935 and the infant mortality rate fell from 159 to 58 per thousand. In York the infant mortality rate fell from 161 per thousand in 1899 to 55 in 1936; in the same period nearly 2 inches [5 cm] was added to the height of schoolchildren and nearly 5 lbs [2.25 kg] to their weight. Growing prosperity and improving health are facts established for these towns not as general impressions but by scientific impartial investigation. What has been shown for these towns in detail applies to the country generally. The real wages of labour, what the wage-earner could buy with his earnings just before the present war, were in general about one-third higher than in 1900 for an hour less of work each day. What the wage-earner could buy, when earning had been interrupted by sickness, accident or unemployment or had been ended by old age, had increased in even larger proportion, though still inadequately, by development of social insurance and allied services.

The rise in the general standard of living in Britain in the thirty or forty years that ended with the present war has two morals. First, growing general prosperity and rising wages diminished want, but did not reduce want to insignificance. The moral is that new measures to spread prosperity are needed. The Plan for Social Security is designed to meet this need; to establish a national minimum above which prosperity can grow, with want abolished. Second, the period covered by the comparisons between say 1909 and 1936 includes the First World War. The moral is the encouraging one, that it is wrong to assume that the present war must bring economic progress for Britain, or for the rest of the world, to an end. After four years of open warfare and diversion of effort from useful production to the means of destruction during 1914–18, there followed an aftermath of economic conflict; international trade was given no chance to recover from the war, and Britain entered into a period of mass unemployment in her staple industries. Yet, across this waste period of destruction and dislocation, the permanent forces making for material progress – technical advance and the capacity of human society to adjust itself to new conditions – continued to operate; the real wealth per head in a Britain of shrunken overseas investments and lost export markets, counting in all her unemployed, was materially higher in 1938 than in 1913. The present war may be even more destructive. It is likely to complete the work of the first war in exhausting British investments overseas and to deprive Britain largely of another source of earning abroad through shipping services: in these and in other ways it will change the economic environment in which the British people must live and work and may call for radical and in some ways painful readjustments. There are bound to be acute difficulties of transition; there are no easy carefree times in early prospect. But to suppose that the difficulties cannot be overcome, that power of readjustment has deserted the British people, that technical advance has ended or can end, that the British of the future must be permanently poor because they will have spent their fathers' savings, is defeatism without reason and against reason.

The economic argument set out above is in terms not of money, but of standards of living and of real wages. If the argument is sound, it is clear that abolition of want by redistribution of income is within our means. The problem of how the plan should be financed in terms of money is secondary, though it is a real problem, since the fact that the whole burden, properly distributed, could be borne does not mean that it can be borne unless it is distributed wisely. Wise distribution of the burden is the object of the Social Security Budget as outlined in Part IV. There it is shown that the Plan involves for the National Exchequer an additional charge of at most £86 million in the first year of full operation. It does not seem unreasonable to hope that even with the other calls upon the Exchequer, an additional expense of this order could be borne when actual fighting ceases. The Budget imposes a much increased burden on the Exchequer in later years to provide retirement pensions; this is an act of reasonable faith in the future of the British economic system and the proved efficiency of the British people. That, given reasonable time, this burden can be borne is hardly open to question. The exact rate at which the burden will rise is not settled finally in accepting the plan, since the length of the transition period for pensions is capable of adjustment and, if necessary, can be prolonged without serious hardship. As regards the insured person, the Budget requires of him contributions for vital security which together are materially less than he is now paying for compulsory insurance and for voluntary insurance for less important purposes, or on account of medical services for which he pays when he receives them. For the employers, the plan imposes an addition to their costs for labour which should be well repaid by the greater efficiency and content which they secure.

The argument of this section can be summed up briefly. Abolition of want cannot be brought about merely by increasing production, without seeing to correct distribution of the product; but correct distribution does not mean what it has often been taken to mean in the past – distribution between the different agents in production, between land, capital, management and labour. Better distribution of purchasing power is required among wage-earners themselves, as between times of earning and not earning, and between times of heavy family responsibilities and of light or no family responsibilities. Both social insurance and children's allowances are primarily methods of redistributing wealth.

2C   'Subsistence Benefit' Levels and the Problem of Rent

Source: SIAS (1942), pp. 14, 77–85

Social insurance should aim at guaranteeing the minimum income needed for subsistence. What the actual rates of benefit and contribution should be in terms of money cannot be settled now, and that for two reasons. First, it is impossible today to forecast with assurance the level of prices after the war. Second, determination of what is required for reasonable human subsistence is to some extent a matter of judgement; estimates on this point change with time, and generally, in a progressive community, change upwards. The procedure adopted to deal with this problem has been: first, from consideration of subsistence needs, as given by impartial expert authorities, to determine the weekly incomes which would have been sufficient for subsistence in normal cases at prices ruling in 1938; second, to derive from these the rates appropriate to a cost of living about 25 per cent above that of 1938. These rates of benefit, pension and grant are set out in para. 401 as provisional postwar rates; by reference to them it is possible to set forth simply what appears to be the most appropriate relation between different benefits and what would be the cost of each benefit and of all benefits together; it is possible to show benefits in relation to contributions and taxation. But the provisional rates themselves are not essential. If the value of money when the scheme comes into operation differs materially from the assumptions on which the provisional rates are based, the rates could be changed without affecting the scheme in any important particular. If social policy should demand benefits on a higher scale than subsistence, the whole level of benefit and contribution rates could be raised without affecting the structure of the scheme. If social policy or financial stringency should dictate benefits on a lower scale, benefits and contributions could be lowered, though not perhaps so readily or without some adjustments within the scheme.

The most important of the provisional rates is the rate of 40/- [£2] a week for a man and wife in unemployment and disability and after the transition period as retirement pension, in addition to allowances for children at an average of 8/- [40p] per head per week. These amounts represent a large addition to existing benefits. They will mean that in unemployment and disability a man and wife, if she is not working, with two children, will receive 56/- [£2.80] a week without means test so long as unemployment or disability lasts, as compared with the 33/- [£1.65] in unemployment and the 15/- [75p] or 7/6 [37p] in sickness, with additional benefit in some Approved Societies,[4] which they were getting before the war.

Any single estimate, such as is necessary for the determination of a rate of insurance benefit, cannot fit exactly the differing conditions of differing households; while the main differences in the cost of living arise through variation of rents, there are differences also in the cost of fuel and other articles. The calculations made have been prepared in consultation with a Subcommittee including Professor A. L. Bowley, Mr Seebohm Rowntree, Mr R. F. George and Dr H. E.

Magee, and in respect of items other than rent, have been approved by the Subcommittee as affording a reasonable basis for fixing rates of unemployment and disability benefits which at 1938 prices would provide a subsistence minimum in normal cases. In regard to rent, the Subcommittee express the view that no single figure can be justified on scientific grounds as fitting the needs.

In considering the minimum income needed by persons of working age for subsistence during interruption of earnings, it is sufficient to take into account food, clothing, fuel, light and household sundries, and rent, though some margin must be allowed for inefficiency in spending. Food and rent are the main items of expenditure.

For food it is possible to make estimates on the basis of dietaries. At 1938 prices, it would have been possible to provide an adequate dietary, either on the scale laid down in the 1936 and 1938 Reports of the Technical Commission on Nutrition by the League of Nations or on the scale laid down in 1933 by the Committee on Nutrition of the British Medical Association, for a man and woman together at a cost of about 13/- [65p] a week. Reference to these dietaries does not imply a view that they are themselves incapable of improvement or would be accepted today as final by all authorities. The science of nutrition, like other sciences, progresses and shows how health may be improved by different ways of feeding. But a better dietary is not necessarily a more expensive dietary.

Rent has three characteristics differentiating it from other forms of expenditure:-

(i) Rent varies markedly from one part of the country to another.
(ii) Rent varies markedly as between different families of the same size in the same part of the country.
(iii) Expenditure on rent cannot be reduced during a temporary interruption of earning as that on clothing, fuel or light can.

The average weekly rent paid by all industrial households included in the Ministry of Labour Family Budget in 1937–8 was 10/9 [54p]. If any single figure is to be taken as the prewar requirement for rent in fixing rates of benefit, a figure of 10/- [50p] a week is the natural suggestion. The figure should be below rather than above the average shown in the budgets, since these cover families living well above the subsistence level; the average rents of applicants for unemployment assistance deduced from the table given below for each of the three regions would be appreciably below those shown by the family budgets for those regions. Mr Rowntree by independent enquiry reached 9/6 [47p] a week as the best single figure for rent requirement in 1936. The figure of 10/- [50p] is for a household. For solitary individuals a figure of 6/6 [32p] is taken.

But neither 10/- [50p], nor any other single figure, can fit the true requirements even reasonably well. A glance at Table 1 shows that an allowance of 10/- [50p] a week for rent in 1938 would have been anything from 2/6 [12p] to 7/6 [37p] too much for more than two-thirds of the Scottish households and anything from 2/6 [12p] to 10/- [50p] and upwards too little for half the London households. In no part of the country would it have been within 2/6 [12p] of the actual rent for as many as half the households. It would have been at least twice as much as was needed for more than half the agricultural households. With the present variety of rents, it is not possible to fix any uniform rate of insurance benefit as meeting subsistence requirements with any accuracy. Even when differences in the size of the family have been provided for by allowances for dependants, any uniform rate must be many shillings a week too high for many cases and many shillings too low for many other cases.

Table 2.1 *Distribution of Rents Paid by Applicants for Unemployment Assistance, 1938*

rent	Free to 2/5	2/6 to 4/11	5/- to 7/5	7/6 to 9/11	10/- to 12/5	12/6 to 14/11	15/- to 17/5	17/6 to 19/11	20/- and over
	%	%	%	%	%	%	%	%	%
England and Wales	1.5	8.0	27.5	29.6	17.8	7.3	4.6	1.7	2.0
Scotland	6.6	23.8	39.7	22.7	5.3	1.2	0.4	0.2	0.1
London	0.8	2.0	8.6	14.7	22.6	17.6	15.7	7.2	10.8

Source: Unemployment Assistance Board Report (1938), p. 198

While the difficulties of principle and of practice, in the way of adjusting benefits to individual rents, are probably sufficient to justify rejection of this proposal, the difficulty of meeting the differing requirements of households by a uniform rate of benefit in all parts of the country remains. The difficulty presents itself in regard to benefits and contributions alike. A rate of benefit adequate for needs, where rents are high, will be more than adequate for regions of low rent, and will involve contributions that may appear excessive in relation to the wages earned.

2D   The Nature of Social Insurance and its Rationale

Source: SIAS (1942), pp. 11–12

Under the scheme of social insurance, which forms the main feature of this plan, every citizen of working age will contribute in his appropriate class according to the security that he needs, or as a married woman will have contributions made by the husband. Each will be covered for all his needs by a single weekly contribution on one insurance document. All the principal cash payments – for unemployment, disability and retirement – will continue so long as the need lasts, without means test, and will be paid from a Social Insurance Fund built up by contributions from the insured persons, from their employers, if any, and from the State. This is in accord with two views as to the lines on which the problem of income maintenance should be approached.

The first view is that benefit in return for contributions, rather than free allowances from the State, is what the people of Britain desire. This desire is shown both by the established popularity of compulsory insurance, and by the phenomenal growth of voluntary insurance against sickness, against death and for endowment, and most recently for hospital treatment. It is shown in another way by the strength of popular objection to any kind of means test. This objection springs not so much from a desire to get everything for nothing, as from resentment at a provision which appears to penalize what people have come to regard as the duty and pleasure of thrift, of putting pennies away for a rainy day. Management of one's income is an essential element of a citizen's freedom. Payment of a substantial part of the cost of benefit as a contribution irrespective of the means of the contributor is the firm basis of a claim to benefit irrespective of means.

The second view is that whatever money is required for provision of insurance benefits, so long as they are needed, should come from a Fund to which the recipients have contributed and to which they may be required to make larger contributions if the Fund proves inadequate. The plan adopted since 1930 in regard to prolonged unemployment and sometimes suggested for prolonged disability, that the State should take this burden off insurance, in order to keep the contribution down, is wrong in principle. The insured persons should not feel that income for idleness, however caused, can come from a bottomless purse. The Government should not feel that by paying doles it can avoid the major responsibility of seeing that unemployment and disease are reduced to the minimum. The place for direct expenditure and organization by the State is in maintaining employment of the labour and other productive resources of the country, and in preventing and combating disease, not in patching an incomplete scheme of insurance.

The State cannot be excluded altogether from giving direct assistance to individuals in need, after examination of their means. However comprehensive an insurance scheme some, through physical infirmity, can never contribute at all and some will fall through the meshes of any insurance. The making of insurance benefit without means test unlimited in duration involves of itself that conditions must be imposed at some stage or another as to how men in receipt of benefit shall use their time, so as to fit themselves or to keep themselves fit for service; imposition of any condition means that the condition may not be fulfilled and that a case of assistance may arise. Moreover for one of the main purposes of social insurance – provision for old age or retirement – the contributory principle implies contribution for a substantial number of years; in the introduction of adequate contributory pensions there must be a period of transition during which those who have not qualified for pension by contribution but are in need have their needs met by assistance pensions. National assistance is an essential subsidiary method in the whole Plan for Social Security, and the work of the Assistance Board shows that assistance subject to means test can be administered with sympathetic justice and discretion taking full account of individual circumstances. But the scope of assistance will be narrowed from the beginning and will diminish throughout the transition period for pensions. The scheme of social insurance is designed of itself when in full operation to guarantee the income needed for subsistence in all normal cases.

2E 'Comparisons with Other Countries': Flat Rate versus Graduated Schemes

Source: SIAS (1942), Appendix F, pp. 287–93

Since social security is a common interest of all peoples in the world and since in the past fifty years or so this interest has led nearly everywhere to the development of national institutions of various kinds for the solution of common problems, some of the principal points of similarity or differences between the schemes of different countries are noted briefly here. Tables provided by the International Labour Office show, in general terms, the extent to which the main risks of social insecurity are covered in countries other than Britain. Taking all the 30 countries together, 20 have compulsory sickness insurance, 24 have some form of contributory pensions, 8 have unemployment insurance. Three countries only in the 30 – New Zealand, Bulgaria and Poland – make provision against all the three risks of sickness, old age and unemployment. That is to say, three countries only aim at covering all the principal forms of social insecurity as fully as Britain. The United States has no sickness insurance; Germany has now no unemployment insurance.

Though in the tables an indication is given of the amount of the cash benefits in relation to wages or family income, it is not easy from this to make comparisons between the real value of the cash benefits being paid in Britain or proposed under the plan, and those of other countries. These tables are of interest mainly as illustrating one outstanding difference between the practice of other countries and the practice of Britain both in the past and in the plan proposed. Difficulty of direct comparison of amounts of benefit is due not merely to difficulties in determining the money rates of wages and the real value of wages, but to the difference of principle in fixing the amounts of benefit or pension. In Britain these amounts are flat rates irrespective of earnings, and so are the same for all classes of persons, though with a differentiation for sex in some cases and a differentiation between various forms of interruption of earnings. In most other countries the benefits are percentages of the wages, and vary, therefore, from one man to another. There is no general rate with which the British flat rate can be compared. Looking at it from the other side, the British flat rate cannot be expressed as a percentage of wages; the percentage would vary, being higher for unskilled men with relatively low wages than for skilled men with higher wages. The methods of relating benefit to wages in other countries vary. In Germany the insured population is graded by income classes and this plan has been widely followed. In the United States the amount paid for unemployment and pensions is related to the earnings of each individual insured person. In the Soviet Union, the percentage itself varies from man to man with the same wages. In one way or another, in nearly all countries other than Britain, Eire and New Zealand, the man of low earnings, when sick or unemployed or pensioned, normally gets through compulsory insurance a lower payment than a man of higher earnings. He pays, or his employer pays, a lower contribution, also proportionate to his earnings.

The principle adopted in Britain in the past and proposed to be retained for the future is of a flat rate of State insurance benefit for all. The difference between existing schemes in Britain and the proposals for the future is that the rates of benefit proposed for the future are all materially higher than the present ones and aim at full subsistence. Social insurance in Eire began as part of the British system, and though it has developed on its own lines in some ways, particularly in relation to medical treatment, it retains the flat rate principle for cash benefits. New Zealand, like Britain, differs from the other countries in providing benefits without relation to previous earnings. It differs from Britain in two important respects:—

(a) that apart from the contributory pensions which are to reach their full rate in 1968, all the benefits in New Zealand are subject to a means test;

(b) that nearly all the money required for the security scheme in New Zealand is raised by an income tax, adjusted to capacity to pay. In contrast to this, the British systems, both present and proposed, raise funds partly by flat contribution irrespective of earnings and partly by taxation adjusted to capacity to pay.

The existing schemes of social insurance in Britain, in common with the schemes of most other countries, are schemes for employees rather than for all citizens. They make less provision than is made in a good many other countries for medical treatment of others than the insured persons and of the insured persons themselves, for maternity of women who are gainfully occupied and for funerals. On the other hand their total range is greater than that of nearly all other countries. British social insurance, with its allied services, has merits which are summarized by the International Labour Office in the following terms:–

> The existing British system 'excels in point of (1) its scheme of unemployment insurance, embracing practically the entire employed population, including agricultural workers; (2) its contributory pensions, comparatively adequate as basic pensions, and granted after a comparatively short qualifying period, at comparatively small cost to insured person or employer; (3) its unemployment and old age assistance, nationally financed, guaranteeing a tolerable standard of subsistence, and adjusted to the needs of each individual; (4) the continuity of its medical benefit, granted, from the first day of insurance, during employment, sickness, unemployment, disablement and old age'.

The Plan for Social Security in the Report develops the existing British schemes in four directions: it unifies them while providing for variety of benefit and administration where difference is justified; it extends the scope of insurance to all citizens; it raises benefits to subsistence level and makes them adequate in time; it gives new benefits. While doing this, the plan preserves the main feature of the British system which distinguishes both it and the New Zealand system from the systems of nearly all other countries. This feature is the preservation of a flat rate of benefit not varying with the earnings which have been lost. In planning for social security each country, while it may with advantage learn from the experience of others, needs a scheme adapted to its special conditions and its dominant political ideas. The principle adopted by most other countries of making State insurance benefits proportionate to the earnings which have been lost has advantages and disadvantages. Apart from the greater administrative difficulties, the view taken here is that a system on this principle would not achieve the purposes which for the British people are most important. The reasons for this view may be summarized briefly as follows:–

(1) The flat rate of benefit treating all alike is in accord with British sentiment for equal treatment of all in social insurance, irrespective both of their previous earnings and of the degree of their risk of unemployment or sickness.

(2) A flat rate of benefit, if raised, as it is raised in the proposals of

the Report, to subsistence level, is a direct contribution to a policy of a national minimum. Benefits which are proportions of wages do not guarantee subsistence, and are liable in the case of the lower paid workers to be below subsistence level.

(3) Provision by compulsory insurance of a flat rate of benefit up to subsistence level leaves untouched the freedom and the responsibility of the individual citizen in making supplementary provision for himself above that level. This accords both with the conditions of Britain, where voluntary insurance, particularly against sickness, is highly developed, and with British sentiment. But to give the fullest possible encouragement to voluntary insurance and saving, it is important to reduce to a minimum the cases in which assistance has to be given subject to consideration of means. To do this is a central feature of the plan for Britain as set out in the Report.

2F Conditions for Long-Term Claimants and the Need for Full Employment

Source: SIAS (1942), pp. 57–9, 163–4

The existing provisions for dealing with prolonged interruption of earnings are unsatisfactory. For disability the cash benefit is drastically reduced, though the needs have almost certainly increased; for unemployment the insured person is referred from benefit to assistance, which may give him higher, or lower, or equal income, but will give it subject to a means test, and normally will do nothing but give an income. The needs of persons suffering from prolonged unemployment or disability are, on the one hand, for as much income at least as before, without any means test discouraging voluntary provision, and on the other hand, for the taking of steps to prevent deterioration and encourage recovery. It is proposed, accordingly, that the rates both for unemployment and for disability should continue without diminution so long as unemployment or disability lasts.

To reduce the income of an unemployed or disabled person, either directly or by application of a means test, because the unemployment or disability has lasted for a certain period, is wrong in principle. But it is equally wrong to ignore the fact that to make unemployment or disability benefit, which is adequate for subsistence, also indefinite in duration involves a danger against which practical precautions must be taken. Most men who have once gained the habit of work would rather work – in ways to which they are used – than be idle, and all men would rather be well than ill. But getting work or getting well may involve a change of habits, doing something that is unfamiliar or leaving one's friends or making a painful effort of some other kind. The danger of providing benefits, which are both adequate in amount and indefinite in duration, is that men, as creatures who adapt themselves to circumstances, may settle down to them. In the proposals of the present Report, not only are insurance benefits being made for the first time adequate for subsistence without other means, but the possibility of drawing them is being extended to new classes not hitherto accustomed to industrial discipline. The correlative of the State's undertaking to ensure adequate benefit for unavoidable interruption of earnings, however long, is enforcement of the citizen's obligation to seek and accept all reasonable opportunities of work, to co-operate in measures designed to save him from habituation to idleness, and to take all proper measures to be well. The higher the benefits provided out of a common fund for unmerited misfortune, the higher must be the citizen's sense of obligation not to draw upon that fund unnecessarily.

This general principle leads to the following practical conclusions:

(i) Men and women in receipt of unemployment benefit cannot be allowed to hold out indefinitely for work of the type to which they are used or in their present places of residence, if there is work which they could do available at the standard wage for that work.

(ii) Men and women who have been unemployed for a certain period should be required as a condition of continued benefit to attend a work or training centre, such attendance being designed both as a means of preventing habituation to idleness and as a means of improving capacity for earning. Incidentally, though this is an altogether minor reason for the proposal, such a condition is the most effective way of unmasking the relatively few persons who may be suspected of malingering, who have perhaps some concealed means of earning which they are combining with an appearance of unemployment. The period after which attendance should be required need not be the same at all times or for all persons. It might be extended in times of high unemployment and reduced in times of good employment; six months for adults would perhaps be a reasonable average period of benefit without conditions. But for young persons who have not yet the habit of continuous work the period should be shorter; for boys and girls there should ideally be no unconditional benefit at all; their enforced abstention from work should be made an occasion of further training.

(iii) The measures for control of claims to disability benefit – both by certification and by sick visiting – will need to be strengthened, in view of the large increases proposed in the scale of compulsory insurance benefit and the possibility of adding to this substantially by voluntary insurance through friendly societies.

(iv) Special attention should be paid to the prevention of chronic disability, by intensified treatment, advice and supervision of cases in which it is threatened and by research into its causes.

(v) Conditions imposed on benefit must be enforced where necessary by suitable penalties.

The practicability of adopting the principle of special treatment for prolonged disability depends on adequate development of the medical service (Assumption B). Practicability of the same thing in regard to unemployment depends on the satisfaction of Assumption C, that is to say, on maintenance of employment to keep within reasonable numbers the men who are likely to exhaust unconditional benefit.

There are five reasons for saying that a satisfactory scheme of social insurance assumes the maintenance of employment and the prevention of mass unemployment. Three reasons are concerned with the details of social insurance; the fourth and most important is concerned with its principle; the fifth is concerned with the possibility of meeting its cost.

First, payment of unconditional cash benefits as of right during unemployment is satisfactory provision only for short periods of unemployment; after that, complete idleness even on an income demoralizes. The proposal of the Report accordingly is to make unemployment benefit after a certain period conditional upon attendance at a work or training centre. But this proposal is impracticable, if it has to be applied to men by the million or the hundred thousand.

Second, the only satisfactory test of unemployment is an offer of work. This test breaks down in mass unemployment and makes necessary recourse to elaborate contribution conditions, and such devices as the Anomalies Regulations[5], all of which should be avoided in a satisfactory scheme of unemployment insurance.

Third, the state of the labour market has a direct bearing on rehabilitation and recovery of injured and sick persons and upon the possibility of giving to those suffering from partial infirmities, such as deafness, the chance of a happy and useful career. In time of mass unemployment those who are in receipt of compensation feel no urge to get well. On the other hand, in time of active demand for labour, as in war, the sick and maimed are encouraged to recover, so that they may be useful.

Fourth, and most important, income security which is all that can be given by social insurance is so inadequate a provision for human happiness that to put it forward by itself as a sole or principal measure of reconstruction hardly seems worth doing. It should be accompanied by an announced determination to use the powers of the State to whatever extent may prove necessary to ensure for all, not indeed absolute continuity of work, but a reasonable chance of productive employment.

Fifth, though it should be within the power of the community to bear the cost of the whole Plan for Social Security, the cost is heavy and, if to the necessary cost waste is added, it may become insupportable. Unemployment, both through increasing expenditure on benefit and through reducing the income to bear those costs, is the worst form of waste.

Assumption C does not imply complete abolition of unemployment. In industries subject to seasonal influences, irregularities of work are inevitable; in an economic system subject to change and progress, fluctuations in the fortunes of individual employers or of particular industries are inevitable; the possibility of controlling completely the major alternations of good trade and bad trade which are described under the term of the trade cycle has not been established; a country like Britain, which must have exports to pay for its raw materials, cannot be immune from the results of changes of fortune or of economic policy in other countries. The Plan for Social Security provides benefit for a substantial volume of unemployment. In the industries now subject to unemployment insurance, the finance of the Unemployment Fund has been based by the Unemployment Insurance Statutory Committee on the assumption of an average rate of unemployment through good years and bad of about 15 per cent. In framing the Social Security Budget in Part IV of this Report, it has been assumed that, in the industries now subject to insurance, the average rate of unemployment will in future be about 10 per cent, and that over the whole body of insured employees in Class I unemployment will average about 8.5 per cent. It is right to hope that unemployment can be reduced to below that level, in which case more money will be available in the Social Insurance Fund either for better benefits or for reduction of contributions. But it would not be prudent to assume any lower rate of unemployment in preparing the Security Budget. Assumption C requires not the abolition of all unemployment, but the abolition of mass unemployment and of unemployment prolonged year after year for the same individual. In the beginning of compulsory unemployment insurance in 1913 and 1914, it was found that less than 5 per cent of all the unemployment experienced in the insured industries occurred after men had been unemployed for as long as 15 weeks. Even if it does not prove possible to get back to that level of employment, it should be possible to make unemployment of any individual for more than 26 weeks continuously a rare thing in normal times.

3

The Development of Social Insurance as a Technique of Welfare

By 1942, Beveridge had been an advocate of social insurance for more than thirty years. But his position on the proper form and scope of the technique had changed significantly over this period. The scheme of social insurance proposed in *SIAS* in 1942 was very different from that which had been originally recommended in *Unemployment* in 1909. The extracts in this chapter are designed to illustrate the development of Beveridge's position on social insurance in the decades before 1942 and in the years immediately afterwards. If Beveridge was an enthusiast for the principle of social insurance, it is also true that he often had serious reservations about the practice of social insurance in Britain after 1911. In this case, the social reformer's vision of what ought to be, sharpened his criticism of what was. Thus, the extracts are also designed to illustrate Beveridge's reservations about the development of unemployment insurance in the 1920s and about the implementation of the Beveridge Report in the early and mid-1940s.

Beveridge's changes of position on social insurance were not the result of a process of intellectual auto-genesis. They form a commentary on a world where the technique of social insurance carried all before it once it had been 'invented' in Germany in 1883 and introduced into Britain in 1911. Any examination of numbers insured and benefits paid out in Britain in the thirty years before 1942, show how insurance created the modern field of income maintenance.

Total numbers enrolled in separate social insurance schemes for unemployment, sickness and old age

	unemployment	sickness	widows', orphans', old age pensions	gross enrolment
	million	million	million	million
1914	2.5	13.7		16.2
1921	11.1	15.2		26.3
1931	12.5	17.4	18.5	48.4
1938	15.4	19.7	20.7	55.8

Source: SIAS (1942), p. 213

In 1900–1, when only out-relief and workmen's compensation was available, some £4 million was paid out for these items. By 1938–9, with contributory social insurance dominant in the areas of unemployment, sickness and old age pensions, the income maintenance pay-out was some £236 million.

In general terms this outcome in Britain, as elsewhere, was guaranteed by the fiscal efficiency of the technique of social insurance which could put income maintenance on a largely self-financing basis. In the interwar period most of what was paid out as insurance benefit came from employee and employer contributions to the insurance fund rather than from the exchequer and national taxation. The state's share of insurance expenditure on sickness benefit and pensions was set at one-sixth. Self-financing unemployment insurance was more problematic when there was always a standing army of 1 million unemployed; but, even here, the state never covered much more than one-third of the expenditure. It was never possible to abolish assistance which came initially out of the rates and subsequently from general taxation. But a substantial part of the combined cost of insurance and assistance was met by employer and employee contributions; Beveridge calculated (SIAS, 1942, p. 214) that in 1938–9 46 per cent of the combined cost of insurance and assistance was covered by insurance contributions.

The introduction of social insurance became inevitable before 1914 when the Liberal government showed no interest in grand schemes of tutelage and embarked on a cautious strategy of giving very limited sums of money to the poor; the schemes for old age, unemployment and sickness all centred on small cash doles (see, for example, Harris, 1977). At a national level, the revenue from existing forms of taxation was already fully committed. The provision of non-contributory old age pensions in 1908 was only possible thanks to the accident of a pause in naval building. At a local level, the system of poor relief assistance from the rates had reached its limits before 1914. This point was proved in the 1920s when the poor law unions in high unemployment areas had to be relieved of the burden of maintaining the long unemployed. Before 1914 the poor law had played a major role in maintaining the elderly: one-third of all old people claimed out-relief in the course of a year in the 1900s. But the number of old people was increasing rapidly. In 1901 there were 2 million old people (men over 65 and women over 60); by 1941 there were 5 million old people who accounted for one in eight of the whole population. Contributory old age pensions were introduced in 1925 because for the old, as for other groups, the provision of income maintenance depended on contributions.

If the general triumph of insurance in the new field of income maintenance was inevitable, there was much scope for contemporary debate and real differences about the specific form and scope of social insurance which was appropriate in particular circumstances. Beveridge was an active participant in these debates for more than thirty years as a freelance 'expert' and academic commentator on insurance. More than this, he was also an official participant in the design and redesign of social insurance schemes as a civil servant at the Board of Trade after 1908 and then as chairman of the quango Unemployment Insurance Committee[1] after 1934. This career in social insurance culminated in his 1941 appointment to chair the interdepartmental committee which produced *SIAS*.

The health and unemployment insurance schemes established by the 1911 Insurance Act provided a framework for the subsequent development of social insurance; they introduced the principles of compulsory tripartite contributions for flat rate benefits. But, for Beveridge and others, when social insurance was introduced before 1914 it was not seen as a general or universal technique of welfare. This was especially so for the unemployment insurance which was Beveridge's primary concern in this period. In both majority and minority reports of the 1909 Royal Commission[2] the technique of insurance was set in a distinctive Edwardian problematic where it figured as one amongst a battery of policy instruments which could be used to deal with different kinds of unemployment. The senior civil servant responsible for unemployment insurance took a similar position; the task was to construct a scheme which 'shall automatically discriminate as between the classes of unemployment for which insurance is or is not an appropriate remedy' (extract 3A). This discrimination was achieved by restricting coverage and benefit levels and by establishing fierce contributory conditions. The scheme of 1911 covered just 2.25 million mainly skilled workers in selected trades and offered a benefit of 7/- (35p) a week which was one-third of the average unskilled wage of around £1 a week. Such benefits could only be drawn by those who satisfied the contributory conditions; five contributions were necessary for one benefit and a maximum of 15 weeks benefit could be drawn in one year. As extract 3A shows the contributory conditions had a simple, conscious rationale; 'armed with this double weapon of a maximum limit to benefit and of a minimum contribution, the operation of the scheme itself will automatically exclude the loafer'. The newly created labour exchanges[3] provided a further safeguard against imposition; the genuineness of unemployment could be tested with the offer of a job.

This preoccupation with excluding the 'loafer' is intelligible in its historical context. The poor law had deliberately moved out of assistance to the unemployed in mid-Victorian Britain (Williams, 1981). Without recent experience of a dole system for the unemployed, there were fears that any assistance would demoralize them. Against this background, Beveridge was able to represent the state's movement back into the business of assisting the unemployed as 'a daring adventure' (extract 3A). It could perhaps be more fairly described as a cautious experiment which extended the trade union unemployment insurance cover already enjoyed by many of the skilled. The limited coverage and strict contribution rules ensured that the new state scheme never offered benefit to any long-term unemployed or to the underemployed 'casual' labourers whose distress had featured prominently in discussions of the social problems since the 1880s. In their 1911 book on unemployment Rowntree and Lasker demonstrated the substantial irrelevance of the new state scheme; the 15-week time limit on drawing benefit was alone sufficient to ensure that half the York unemployed would be ineligible. Our argument so far shows how and why this kind of irrelevance was designed into the scheme. The original unemployment insurance scheme of 1911 found its natural object in providing aid for that group of the regularly employed who worked in cyclical trades and suffered short spells of unemployment when the economy turned down. For such workers the scheme offered a strictly limited insurance cover.

The original unemployment insurance scheme was judged to be a great success (extract 3A). Its extension to cover larger numbers of workers, subject to the same contributory conditions, was proposed in 1918 by a wartime Reconstruction Subcommittee which Beveridge chaired. The 1920 Insurance Act finally extended the scheme to cover most manual workers. In late 1920 the scheme was also significantly changed by the introduction of dependants' allowances; by this means a family man with a wife and two children could claim an allowance which covered most of his family's subsistence needs. This increased what we would now call the replacement ratio between dole and wages. The scheme which had hitherto operated only in prosperity was then overwhelmed by mass unemployment; the postwar replacement boom turned into general slump in 1921 from which the staple industries in north and west Britain never recovered. When it was politically inexpedient to deny the dole, and when the poor law could not cope, the contributory conditions for insurance benefit were relaxed. By the end of the decade the long unemployed could draw ordinary insurance benefit for nearly eighteen months. Those who exhausted this benefit entitlement could apply for a special kind of non-contributory insurance benefit paid out of the insurance fund subject to conditions such as a household means test and a 'genuinely seeking work' condition. This supplementary entitlement was variously known as 'uncovenanted', 'extended' and 'transitional' benefit. After 1922 more than three-quarters of the unemployed obtained benefit in one form or another (Williams, 1981). Beveridge aptly summarized this development as a movement 'from insurance by contract to relief by status'.

Extract 3B gives Beveridge's verdict on the social and economic effects of a system which made doles available to almost all the unemployed. He accepted the general conclusion of 1920s investigators that doles did not demoralize; as the 'Third Winter Group'[4] concluded in 1923, 'the great discovery that has been made is that a system of allowances by which the worst effects of distress are prevented does not necessarily involve widespread demoralization'. At the same time, Beveridge argued that this was a mixed blessing because 'relief of unemployment is after all a very bad second best to its prevention' (extract 3B). Furthermore, such relief for the unemployed positively hindered the prevention of unemployment because it impeded market clearing wage adjustments (i.e. large cuts in wage levels) and because it limited the political pressure for new policy initiatives. This last point has considerable force. The public works proposals in the 1929 Liberal Yellow Book[5] were not so much intellectually deficient as politically incredible when successive governments could maintain the unemployed cheaply by an insurance contribution levied on the other half of the employed population who were steadily in work.

Mainly because of politically over-optimistic assumptions about future unemployment levels, the unemployed were maintained from an insurance fund which was increasingly in deficit. By the end of the 1920s there was a lively debate about what should be done about the deficit and the Royal Commission on Unemployment Reports of 1931 show how opinion then divided sharply on political lines. The left Minority Report argued for the unemployed's right to maintenance out of progressive direct taxation. The right Majority Report argued for a reassertion of strict contributory insurance principles which would clear many claimants off on to means-tested assistance. In a moderate way, Beveridge then sided with the right. In 1930, he proposed

> giving a limited [insurance] cover against the industrial risk of unemployment, and supplementing insurance by a reformed poor law, which shall provide by a different agency different treatment to those who have run through their claims and manifestly need something more than tiding over by money payments. (*The Past and Present of Unemployment Insurance*, 1930, p. 49)

As this quotation shows, Beveridge's position reflected his conviction that insurance cash benefits were unsuitable for the long-term unemployed and this theme runs through all his discussion of unemployment insurance from 1909 to 1942. For example, in 1924 he wrote that insurance 'can be justified only as a means of tiding over temporary unemployment not as a pension for life' (*Insurance for All and Everything*, 1924, p. 22). Over time, Beveridge slowly changed his views about what needed to be done about those who exhausted their entitlement; by the early 1940s, he was convinced that economic policy could reduce the number of long unemployed so that large numbers would not need to be turned off insurance.

If Beveridge was prepared to contemplate the curbing of insurance doles for the unemployed, from the early 1920s he was also convinced that the insurance principle could be more generally extended. Extract 3C is taken from Beveridge's 1924 pamphlet *Insurance For All and Everything*. For the first time here Beveridge identified insurance as a general technique of welfare which could cover a whole population against 'all the main risks'. Beveridge now argued for

> the completion of social insurance [which] means the remedying of imperfections in particular schemes, the taking in of the one large outstanding risk of widowed motherhood and the welding of all the schemes into one autonomous system without gaps and overlapping. (*Insurance for All and Everything*, 1924, p. 5).

In 1924 this welding together was to take the form of 'co-ordination' rather than 'amalgamation'. Using an Edwardian kind of argument, it was asserted that sickness and unemployment were heterogeneous problems requiring the different administrative apparatuses of panel doctors and labour exchanges.

> The interruptions to earnings with which they [different insurance schemes] deal affect different types of persons and are different in character and probable duration. These differences justify varying scales of benefit and necessitate separate machinery. (extract 3C)

The differences in benefit level proposed in 1924 were considerable; the sick or unemployed single person would get a standard 15/- (75p) benefit but the disabled would get only half that sum and the elderly were to get 10/- (50p) subject to means test for those aged over 70.

Sections of the 1924 pamphlet have been reproduced partly because in many respects it anticipates *SIAS* in 1942 which proposed insurance 'all-embracing in scope of persons and needs'. The problem definition about earnings interruption, for example, is clearly already in place nearly twenty years before *SIAS*. A cursory reading suggests that the later text added only (or mainly) the notion of full subsistence allowances for all. At a deeper level, however, there can be no doubt that the later text does represent a real break. Partly this is so because by 1942 Beveridge proposes a rather different kind of comprehensive insurance; as extract 3D shows, *SIAS* proposes the amalgamation of all insurance schemes into one unified apparatus.

The other significant difference is that *SIAS* establishes an effective connection between social and economic policy via the assumption that government can and will act to curb unemployment. In 1924 Beveridge could only hope piously that 'unemployment will in time return to round the normal figure' (*Insurance for All and Everything*, 1924, p. 36). If we are interested in longer-term comparisons between Edwardian beginnings and 1942, extract 3D from *SIAS* is also of interest because it demonstrates how the role of classification was modified in the later problematic. In Edwardian texts classification was a preliminary intellectual task which involved the discrimination of subgroups for whom insurance was appropriate. In 1942 classification was an administrative principle which defined the individual's status as contributor or beneficiary by means of his (or her) variable relation to the labour market in a world where all would be protected by insurance from the cradle to the grave.

If *SIAS* in 1942 put Beveridge's plans for comprehensive social insurance into nearly definitive form, as we argued in the last chapter, this plan was not an easy one to implement. Beveridge's flat rate proposals created a space where, in administering insurance, the government was constantly tempted to restrict entitlement (in terms of numbers and/or benefit level) so as to ease severe financial constraints. Successive governments did not so much deviate from the Beveridge plan as thrash around in the Beveridge constraints. Extracts 3E and 3F give us Beveridge's commentary on the government's proposals for implementing his scheme in the years 1943 to 1945. They cover all the key issues which emerged during and immediately after implementation – the question of benefit levels and entitlement, the erosion of benefit purchasing power by inflation and the division of the burden of contribution between the three parties (employers, employees and the Treasury).

As extract 3E shows, Beveridge's fundamental complaint was that the government was setting insurance benefits too low and thus the primary objective of 'abolishing want' had been compromised.

> The government in regard to pensions entirely and in regard to children's allowances and to unemployment and disability benefit to a lesser extent abandon that aim. (*Pillars of Security*, 1943, p. 132).

Beveridge also argued that, if the prime motive was 'the need for financial prudence', the government's decisions were not particularly sensible. After the cost of assistance top-up had been allowed for, the lower insurance benefits would ultimately save no more than £30 million a year which might be no more than 0.25 per cent of national income in 1975. If this point was factually correct, it rested on a naive misunderstanding about the politics of old age pensions which would be the major drain on the new insurance fund. Throughout the debate on implementation Beveridge defended the original *SIAS* concept of a scale of old age pensions which would rise as contributions built up over twenty years after 1945. His scheme offered the current generation of pensioners less but the next generation in the 1960s were promised more than 35/- (£1.75) per week which the government offered all pensioner couples in 1945 (extract 3E). It was not surprising that the politicians in the postwar Labour government preferred to offer the current generation of pensioners more and then did not hasten to adjust benefit levels even though postwar inflation eroded the purchasing power of benefits between 1945 and 1951. Successive governments also took a generous line on the right of those with limited contributions to draw full pensions; from 1948 the Labour government paid full old age pensions to all those who had been insured before 1945. In this situation it was inevitable that benefits could not be raised to the levels which Beveridge had recommended and the finances of the insurance fund became increasingly problematic with the Treasury obliged to pay an increasing share of the cost of insurance. The scene was set for the crisis of the early 1950s and the appointment of the Phillips committee.[6]

Extract 3F reprints a neglected piece of journalism from *The Times* of 1945 which gives us Beveridge's last thoughts about how the *SIAS* design of 1945 should be modified. Beveridge here attempts to come to terms with the deficiencies of a flat rate insurance scheme. He conceded the force of the 'scientific criticism' that the flat rate principle and regressive taxation had been simply pushed too far in the 1942 scheme. His defensive response was to maintain the flat rate principle while arguing that the regressive tax burden could be eased by transferring a significant proportion of the costs and risks of social insurance from contributors to the state. For example, in the 1942 report contribution levels had been set on the assumption of 8.5 per cent unemployment for manual workers; in 1945 Beveridge observed that joint employer and employee contributions could be reduced by 1*s* 1*d* (about 5p) if 3 per cent unemployment were assumed and 'the risk of failure to achieve the full employment . . . should be borne by the State' (extract 3F).

The Phillips committee which reported on old age pensions in 1954 came to quite different conclusions. Phillips recommended that the deficiency of the insurance fund should be made good by contributors rather than the Treasury; on this view it was the contributors who should accept a larger share of the risks and costs of insurance. The 1954 Insurance Act which followed fixed the level of exchequer support for the fund at 17 per cent; this was the traditional one-sixth share which the Treasury had paid towards contributory pensions in the 1925–48 period. In a more ideologically explicit way, the Phillips committee also recommended that the government abandon the Beveridge objective of a flat rate insurance pension which would be adequate without other means of support; it concluded that such pensions 'would be an extravagant use of national resources'. *SIAS* in 1942 had raised high expectations which just over a decade later were being officially revised downwards. Within the limits of a flat rate revenue base, it was difficult to do anything else in the 1950s. At the end of this decade, labour pension plans and conservative legislation both bowed to necessity and accepted the principle of graduated, earnings-related contributions and benefits. The struggle for adequate pensions and benefits then moved on to the terrain which we now occupy. To our shame, successive earnings-related schemes have often done little more than use graduated contributions to bail out the finances of flat rate benefit schemes and, on the jam tomorrow principle of our new realistic politics, they have never offered very much to the current generation of pensioners. Beveridge can hardly be blamed for that.

3A 'A Daring Adventure', the Introduction of Unemployment Insurance in 1911

Source: Unemployment: a problem of industry, Part II (1930), pp. 263–71

On 19th May, 1909, Mr Winston Churchill, as President of the Board of Trade, announced the intention of the Government to introduce compulsory insurance against unemployment. The project seemed then and was a daring adventure. Except for one ill-judged and disastrous experiment in the Canton of St Gall, compulsory insurance against unemployment had never been attempted in any country of the world. All voluntary schemes had been immediate failures or insignificant successes. The only working model on a large scale was afforded by trade unions, which undertook no legal liabilities, were armed with almost indefinite powers of raising levies, and consisted predominantly of the picked members of skilled trades . . .

The chief official concerned – Sir Herbert Llewellyn Smith,[7] then Permanent Secretary of the Board of Trade – happened in 1910 to be President of the Economic Section of the British Association, and took the occasion in his Presidential Address to analyse the problem of unemployment insurance and, incidentally, expound the principles underlying the scheme which he with others was framing. The following extract from his address has historical importance, as a record of the hopes, anxieties and purposes with which unemployment insurance came into the world:–

The crucial question from a practical point of view is, therefore, whether it is possible to devise a scheme of insurance which, while nominally covering unemployment due to all causes other than those which can be definitely excluded, shall automatically discriminate as between the classes of unemployment for which insurance is or is not an appropriate remedy.

We can advance a step towards answering this crucial question by enumerating some of the essential characteristics of any unemployment insurance schemes which seem to follow directly or by necessary implication from the conditions of the problem as here laid down.

1   The scheme must be compulsory; otherwise the bad personal risks against which we must always be on our guard would be certain to predominate.

2   The scheme must be contributory, for only by exacting rigorously as a necessary qualification for benefit that a sufficient number of weeks' contributions shall have been paid by each recipient can we possibly hope to put limits on the exceptionally bad risks.

3   With the same object in view there must be a maximum limit to the amount of benefit which can be drawn, both absolutely and in relation to the amount of contribution paid; or, in other words, we must in some way or other secure that the number of weeks for which a workman contributes should bear some relation to his claim upon the fund. Armed with this double weapon of a maximum limit to benefit and of a minimum

contribution, the operation of the scheme itself will automatically exclude the loafer.

4   The scheme must avoid encouraging unemployment, and for this purpose it is essential that the rate of unemployment benefit payable shall be relatively low. It would be fatal to any scheme to offer compensation for unemployment at a rate approximating to that of ordinary wages.

5   For the same reason it is essential to enlist the interest of all those engaged in the insured trades, whether as employers or as workmen, in reducing unemployment, by associating them with the scheme both as regards contribution and management.

6   As it appears on examination that some trades are more suitable to be dealt with by insurance than others, either because the unemployment in these trades contains a large insurable element, or because it takes the form of total discharge rather than short time, or for other reasons, it follows that, for the scheme to have the best chance of success, it should be based upon the trade group, and should at the outset be partial in operation.

7   The group of trades to which the scheme is to be applied must, however, be a large one, and must extend throughout the United Kingdom, as it is essential that industrial mobility as between occupations and districts should not be unduly checked.

8   A State subvention and guarantee will be necessary, in addition to contributions from the trades affected, in order to give the necessary stability and security, and also in order to justify the amount of State control that will be necessary.

9   The scheme must aim at encouraging the regular employer and workman, and discriminating against casual engagements. Otherwise it will be subject to the criticism of placing an undue burden on the regular for the benefit of the irregular members of the trade.

10   The scheme must not act as a discouragement to voluntary provision for unemployment, and for that purpose some well-devised plan of co-operation is essential between the State organization and the voluntary associations which at present provide unemployment benefit for their members.

Our analysis, therefore, leads us step by step to the contemplation of a national contributory scheme of insurance universal in its operation within the limits of a large group of trades – a group so far as possible self-contained and carefully selected as favourable for the experiment, the funds being derived from compulsory contributions from all those engaged in these trades, with a subsidy and guarantee from the State, and the rules relating to benefit being so devised as to discriminate effectively against unemployment which is mainly due to personal defects, while giving a substantial allowance to those whose unemployment results from industrial causes beyond the control of the individual.

The analysis leads also, as might be expected, step by step, to a scheme indistinguishable from that which had been announced a year before by Mr Churchill and was embodied a year later in Part II of the National Insurance Act. This scheme combined compulsory contributory insurance for limited benefits in selected trades with subsidies to voluntary insurance through associations in all trades. Its main features may be summarized as follows:–

The compulsorily insured trades were building, construction of works, shipbuilding, mechanical engineering, ironfounding, construction of vehicles and saw milling carried on in connection with any other insured trade or of a kind commonly so carried on. Every workman in those trades had to have an 'unemployment book' which he handed to his employer on being engaged, and which the employer gave back to the workman when for any cause the employment ended. To this book the employer had for each week of employment to affix a *5d* [2p] insurance stamp, and was entitled to deduct half the value, that is 2.*5d* [1p], from the workman's wages . . . [The State contribution was one-third of the sum received from employers and workmen, that is to say, roughly 1.66*d* [0.6p] a week, or one-fourth of the whole . . . The benefit was 7*s* [35p] a week up to a maximum of fifteen weeks in a year, subject to the provisos that no one should get more than one week of benefit for every five contributions paid or deemed to have been paid for him, and that no benefit would be paid for the first week of any period of unemployment.]

After its announcement by Mr Churchill in 1909, the scheme was not formally introduced till 1911, when it appeared as Part II of the National Insurance Bill . . . Contributions became payable from 15th July, 1912, and benefits six months later. The scheme was thus fully launched on 15th January, 1913. It took the water smoothly and found smooth water to receive it; the eighteen months from the beginning of 1913 to the outbreak of the Great War were a time of exceptional prosperity and of unemployment as low as had been known for a generation . . . The main features in this year and a half of opening experience may be summarized as follows:–

1 The actual number of insured workpeople proved to be below expectation, about 2.25 million in place of over 2.5 million. The deficiency arose mainly because the building trade was found not to have grown since 1901 at the rate expected; since the building

trade was also expected to have the heaviest unemployment of the insured trades, this was a difference favourable to the finance of the scheme.

2   The contributions materially exceeded the expenditure, and by August, 1914, a surplus of £3,185,000 had been realized. The probable loss in a severe depression, such as that of 1908 and 1909, was estimated at no more than £5,000,000; the fund was already well on the way to security.

3   The number of claims made amounted to nearly 1,100,000, or an average of 20,000 a week, in the insurance year 1913–14; the 1,100,000 claims represented about 550,000 individuals. This meant that, in a year of exceptional prosperity, one out of every four men in the insured trades became unemployed at some time or other, and that there was one claim for every two insured persons. Most of the claimants, however, remained out of work for very short periods. Of the total unemployment experienced only 55 per cent ranked for benefit; over 24 per cent fell in the first week or 'waiting time', in another 17 per cent the workman was disqualified for various reasons, and less than 4 per cent occurred after benefit had been exhausted. Forty claimants out of every 100 got work again in a week and another 35 in three weeks.

3B   'From Insurance by Contract to Relief by Status': Unemployment Insurance in the 1920s

Source: Unemployment: a problem of industry, Part II (1930), pp. 288–94.

Unemployment insurance as introduced, was in two senses contractual. First, it gave the insured person legally enforceable rights without ministerial discretion and without regard to his other sources or private character. Second, it gave these rights in consideration of contributions by or in respect of the insured person . . . During the ten-year chaos from 1918 to 1928 unemployment insurance ceased to be contractual in either sense: donation and extended benefit were discretionary grants and irrespective of contributions by the recipient. Since the Act of 1927 unemployment insurance has become contractual again in the first sense but not in the second; an unlimited benefit claimable as of right has replaced the old combination of standard and extended benefit, but is claimable, not for contributions paid, but by virtue of belonging to the insured classes. Moving from contract to status, the insurance scheme of 1911 has become a general system of outdoor relief of the able-bodied, administered by a national in place of a local authority, and financed mainly by a tax on employment.

With the repeal of the provision for special schemes [of insurance for specific industries] and the making of benefit unlimited in time, following on the disappearance in 1924 of the refund at sixty [for good risks], unemployment insurance has become an insurance in which every attempt to adjust premiums to risks or, conversely, to relate the cover afforded to the premiums paid, has been abandoned. The difference between the Blanesburgh Committee[8] and the advocate of unlimited non-contributory insurance is simply a difference as to modes of taxation: the compulsory contributions have a fiscal significance alone.

The new model of 1927 cannot be defended by the old arguments of 1911. Can it be defended at all? Is it a necessary and serviceable portion of social structure, to be maintained indefinitely, or is it fraught with dangers which only drastic reconstruction can remove? That there are some dangers in unemployment insurance today no unimpassioned observer would deny. But those dangers are not to be found where the most impassioned critics of the scheme now place them.

The main danger of the present situation does not lie in the temptation to individual malingering, that is to say, in the possibility of inducing workpeople to draw benefit when they could get work. This kind of abuse could be stopped completely and at once by employers notifying vacancies promptly and universally to the exchanges; if that were done, no man could draw benefit for a single day on which suitable work was available for him. Even with their present limited control of the labour market, the exchanges as a rule are able to check individual malingering with fair effectiveness.

Through all the transformations of insurance one element endures; one weapon has been added since 1911 to the permanent armoury for dealing with distress. Administration of benefit, in all its forms – standard, extended, donation – has shown the possibility through a labour exchange system of controlling assistance of the unemployed sufficiently to prevent any serious abuse. Charges that the 'dole' was helping numbers of men to live in idleness when they could get work have been made incessantly in the Press, by local authorities, by public men. Whenever they have been investigated, they have been shown to be idle and irresponsible talk. The conclusions of the Committee under the chairmanship of Lord Aberconway which investigated the working of the donation scheme in 1919, have been mentioned already. The Blanesburgh Committee gave the critics another chance.

> Throughout the enquiry we have constantly had brought to our notice the conviction held by many that the system of unemployment insurance is subject to widespread abuses. It has accordingly been one of our principal preoccupations to ascertain how far this belief is justified . . . It is convenient to state at once the conclusion we have reached in this matter. It is true that a certain number out of the 11.75 million of insured persons have received relief to which they had no claim. But it is equally true that these cases are relatively few and that result is, we think, due to the vigilance with which the Ministry, while dealing fairly with the geniune claimant, guards against abuse.

The Secretary of the Charity Organisation Society[9] says that he began by thinking the abuses serious, but, on enquiry, had been unable to find them.

> When this material [i.e. that included in their memorandum] was read to our people on Monday afternoon last, they were much disappointed at the general character of almost all of it. They had hoped that many more examples would be forthcoming illustrating the criticisms passed upon the present working of unemployment insurance by almost everybody who discusses the subject. This shows the value of bringing these criticisms to the test of demanding examples, and more than one of our secretaries said that they quite expected to find from our case-papers numerous examples of abuses, but when they came to look they found very few. This does not, of course, prove that their previous impression was not a sound one; on the other hand, it may quite well prove that unfavourable instances impress themselves upon the memory, while the proper and smooth working of a scheme passes almost unnoticed.

Nor does such a conclusion mean that all the expenditure under the new insurance scheme is necessary or socially desirable. Manifestly some of the benefits go to meet needs of no great urgency and sometimes the scheme is subject to scarcely veiled manipulation by employers and workmen in concert. But if all other critics could be got to emulate both the care and the candour of the Charity Organisation Society, the way would be cleared for seeing where the real dangers of today's unemployment insurance scheme lie and do not lie.

Those dangers, in a sentence, lie not so much in the risk of demoralizing recipients of relief, so that they do not look for work, as in the risk of demoralizing Governments, employers, and trade unions so that they take less thought for the prevention of unemployment.

Relief of unemployment is after all a very bad second best to its prevention; however the giving of money during involuntary idleness be hedged round with safeguards, the idleness itself is demoralizing, and becomes swiftly more demoralizing the longer it lasts. The arguments advanced in 1909, for insurance rather than artificial work as a means of relieving the unemployed, assumed transient depressions, not the chronic underemployment of the casual labourer or the five-year idleness of the derelict coalminer. But once it is admitted in principle, that, either under the guise of insurance or in some other form, genuine unemployment can be relieved indefinitely by the simple device of giving money from a bottomless purse, prevention is only too likely to go by the board. The thoughts and time of Governments and Parliaments may be absorbed – as they have largely been absorbed during the past ten years – in successive extensions and variations of the relief scheme. The fear of causing unemployment may vanish from the minds of trade union negotiators and open the way to excessive rigidity of wages and so to the creation of unemployment. Industries practising casual engagement or perpetual short time may settle down to batten on the taxation of other industries or of the general public in place of reforming their ways. The immobilizing influence of generous employment relief upon the recipient can be controlled by labour exchange machinery, simply and as completely as we choose. For its immobilizing influence on the minds of Governments and leaders of industry the remedies needed are stronger and may be painful.

3C 'The Co-ordination of Insurance': Beveridge's Position in 1924

> Source: *Insurance for All and Everything* (1924), pp. 4–8, 28–31
> (*Insurance for All and Everything* was a short pamphlet published under the auspices of the *Daily News* in 1924.)

There are many possible causes of such interruption [of earnings] at the present time; many causes which may make it impossible for the citizen and householder, through no fault of his own, to fulfil his responsibilities . . .

The first is industrial accident, the sudden misfortune in the course of employment which may mean a week's disablement or may cripple for life or destroy life itself.

The second is sickness, bringing temporary or prolonged incapacity for work before old age is reached.

The third is unemployment – inability to find work for wages though one is anxious to do so and capable of work if found. Before the reports of the Poor Law Commission in 1909, it was common enough to hear the suggestion that unemployment consisted wholly or mainly of the idleness of the unemployable. Now this view is finally discredited.

The fourth is old age. The need to spend and to consume persists to the end of human life, however long. Earning power, even without specific disease, usually stops before then.

The fifth is widowed motherhood . . .

In all these five ways, by industrial accident, sickness, unemployment, old age, or by the death of the breadwinner, the income of the family through current earning may be destroyed permanently or for a time.

In the last years before the war the collective bearing of the risks inherent in modern society – the principle of social insurance – made rapid headway. Compensation for industrial accidents, which had been introduced for a few industries in 1897, was made practically universal in 1906, and old age pensions followed in 1908. Compulsory insurance against sickness, with its new device of contributions paid by stamps and deductions from the workmen's wages, came in 1911. It was accompanied by compulsory insurance against unemployment, also on contributory lines; begun for a few industries in 1911, this, too, was made nearly universal in 1920.

The introduction and acceptance of the principle of contributory insurance, in the last two-named schemes, are notable. The term 'insurance' has been defined above as meaning no more than the collective bearing of risks and has thus been applied both to workmen's compensation and to old age pensions. This is, I think, a justifiable use of the term; we have been familiarized of late with 'free' insurance granted by newspapers to their readers.[10] But it can hardly be doubted that in common thought insurance implies as a rule previous payment of specific premiums by the insured person; the schemes of 1911 dealing with health and unemployment are insurance in a fuller sense than were their predecessors. They aroused also, it may be remembered, a very serious initial opposition. The householder nearly rose in revolt against the insurance stamp. It was freely prophesied that the workman would rise in revolt against having a card to carry with him and against deductions from his wages. Today contributory insurance has won on its merits. It accords with popular sentiment against giving or getting something for nothing. It saves political parties from temptation to compete in easy promises of higher doles. It has manifest administrative advantages in defining the classes to benefit. It raises money which could hardly be raised otherwise; at the present moment four-fifths of the male workmen of the country are without audible protest suffering a weekly deduction of 1s 2d [6p] from their wages. No better proof could be given of how highly men value security against the economic evils of our time.

In the field of social insurance we have now four distinct systems, which have grown up separately, with different and unrelated principles, scope, machinery, sources of income and scales of benefit.

Insurance against Industrial Accidents in the form of Workmen's Compensation is non-contributory for the workman, the whole cost being met by employers, and is administered, not by the State, but by the employers or the insurance companies who stand behind them. The benefit varies with the wages earned but (except now for fatal accidents) not with the number of dependants. Practically the whole employed population is covered but no one who is not employed.

Insurance against Old Age, in the form of Old Age Pensions at 70, is also non-contributory for the workman, but is paid for and administered directly by the State through the Post Office and local Pensions Committees. The benefit is independent of the recipient's previous earnings and the number of his dependants, but varies according to his present means and may be reduced to nothing.

Insurance against Sickness is contributory, being paid for jointly be employers, workmen, and the State. Its outstanding characteristics are on the side of income, the collection of contributions by insurance stamps and deductions from wages, and on the side of expenditure administration by 'approved societies', independent but strictly controlled. Both contributions and benefits are at flat rates independent of the number of dependants and of the wages earned, subject to a limited differentiation of contribution where the wage is very low. The persons insured are broadly the same as those covered by workmen's compensation, but include a certain number of persons working on their own account, not for employers, and exclude employed persons above a certain income limit.

Insurance against Unemployment is contributory in the same way as health insurance, but employs a different set of cards and stamps and bases the State contribution on a different principle. It is administered directly by the State through the Employment Exchanges. The benefit varies with the number of dependants. The scope is narrower than that of accident and health insurance through the omission of agriculture and domestic service.

The four systems involve at the present time an annual expenditure on benefits and administration of about £110,000,000 in Britain alone. Yet they make between them no provision or insufficient provision for widows and orphans (except where death of the husband is due to industrial accident), for infirmity below the age of 70, for accidents other than industrial ones. They present, at their points of contact, numerous illogical distinctions involving real or fancied hardships. It is small wonder that the cry for co-ordination of social insurance should be in the air.

Yet it is important not to exaggerate the present difficulties or to overestimate the degree of uniformity that can be attained. Co-ordination of the various insurance schemes should not mean amalgamation. The interruptions to earnings with which they deal affect different types of persons and are different in character and probable duration. These differences justify varying scales of benefit and necessitate separate machinery. To take one instance – the approved societies are as little fitted to deal with unemployment insurance as the employment exchanges with sickness; the technical instrument for determining whether the insured risk has arisen is in the one case the doctor or the friendly visitor; in the other case, the employment exchange with its register of jobs available.

Co-ordination means simply that the various schemes should for once be looked at as a whole. Their scales of benefit must bear some relation to one another. Their edges must fit, neither overlapping nor leaving holes through which people can drop undeservedly into destitution. They should be amalgamated only so far as this can be done without harming their efficiency for their specific tasks.

3D The 1942 Plan for Insurance 'All-Embracing in Scope of Persons and of Needs'

Source: SIAS (1942), pp. 9–11

The main provisions of the plan may be summarized as follows:

(i) The plan covers all citizens without upper income limit, but has regard to their different ways of life; it is a plan all-embracing in scope of persons and of needs, but is classified in application.

(ii) In relation to social security the population falls into four main classes of working age and two others below and above working age respectively, as follows:

I   Employees, that is, persons whose normal occupation is employment under contract of service.

II   Others gainfully occupied, including employers, traders and independent workers of all kinds.

III Housewives, that is, married women of working age.

IV   Others of working age not gainfully occupied.

V   Below working age.

VI   Retired above working age.

(iii) The sixth of these classes will receive retirement pensions and the fifth will be covered by children's allowances, which will be paid from the National Exchequer in respect of all children when the responsible parent is in receipt of insurance benefit or pension, and in respect of all children except one in other cases. The four other classes will be insured for security appropriate to their circumstances. All classes will be covered for comprehensive medical treatment and rehabilitation and for funeral expenses.

(iv) Every person in Class I, II or IV will pay a single security contribution by a stamp on a single insurance document each week or combination of weeks. In Class I the employer also will contribute, affixing the insurance stamp and deducting the employee's share from wages or salary. The contribution will differ from one class to another, according to the benefits provided, and will be higher for men than for women, so as to secure benefits for Class III.

(v) Subject to simple contribution conditions, every person in Class I will receive benefit for unemployment and disability; pension on retirement, medical treatment and funeral expenses. Persons in Class II will receive all these except unemployment benefit and disability benefit during the first 13 weeks of disability. Persons in Class IV will receive all these except unemployment and disability benefit. As a substitute for unemployment benefit, training benefit will be available to persons in all classes other than Class I, to assist them to find new livelihoods if their present ones fail. Maternity grant, provision for widowhood and separation and qualification for retirement pensions will be secured to all persons in Class III by virtue of their husbands' contributions; in addition to maternity grant, housewives who take paid work will receive maternity benefit for thirteen weeks to enable them to give up working before and after childbirth.

(vi) Unemployment benefit, disability benefit, basic retirement pension after a transition period, and training benefit will be at the same rate, irrespective of previous earnings. This rate will provide by itself the income necessary for subsistence in all normal cases. There will be a joint rate for a man and his wife who is not gainfully occupied. Where there is no wife or she is gainfully occupied, there will be a lower single rate; where there is no wife but a dependant above the age for children's allowance, there will be a dependant allowance. Maternity benefit for housewives who work also for gain will be at a higher rate than the single rate in unemployment or disability, while their unemployment and disability benefit will be at a lower rate: there are special rates also for widowhood as described below. With these exceptions all rates of benefit will be the same for men and for women. Disability due to industrial accident or disease will be treated like all other disability for the first thirteen weeks; if disability continues thereafter, disability benefit at a flat rate will be replaced by an industrial pension related to the earnings of the individual subject to a minimum and a maximum.

(vii) Unemployment benefit will continue at the same rate without means test so long as unemployment lasts, but will normally be subject to a condition of attendance at a work or training centre after a certain period. Disability benefit will continue at the same rate without means test, so long as disability lasts or till it is replaced by industrial pension, subject to acceptance of suitable medical treatment or vocational training.

(viii)   Pensions (other than industrial) will be paid only on retirement from work. They may be claimed at any time after the minimum age of retirement, that is 65 for men and 60 for women. The rate of pension will be increased above the basic rate if retirement is postponed. Contributory pensions as of right will be raised to the full basic rate gradually during a transition period of twenty years, in which adequate pensions according to needs will be paid to all persons requiring them. The position of existing pensioners will be safeguarded.

(ix)   While permanent pensions will no longer be granted to widows of working age without dependent children, there will be for all widows a temporary benefit at a higher rate than unemployment or disability benefit, followed by training benefit where necessary. For widows with the care of dependent children there will be guardian benefit, in addition to the children's allowances, adequate for subsistence without other means. The position of existing widows on pension will be safeguarded.

(x)   For the limited number of cases of need not covered by social insurance, national assistance subject to a uniform means test will be available.

(xi)   Medical treatment covering all requirements will be provided for all citizens by a national health service organized under the health departments and post-medical rehabilitation treatment will be provided for all persons capable of profiting by it.

(xii)   A Ministry of Social Security will be established, responsible for social insurance, national assistance and encouragement and supervision of voluntary insurance, and will take over, so far as necessary for these purposes, the present work of other Government Departments and of Local Authorities in these fields.

3E   'A Difference of Principle' about the Implementation of the Beveridge Report

Source: *Pillars of Security* (1943), pp. 127–32
    Why I am a Liberal (1945), pp. 77–83

(The first extract reprints material which originally appeared as newspaper articles in the *Observer* and the *Daily Herald* in February and March 1943 when the government had indicated its general intentions with regard to implementing *SIAS*. The second extract reprints part of Beveridge's maiden speech made as a newly elected Liberal MP in 1945 when the joint old age pension had been fixed at 35 shillings [£1.75p].)

The Government proposals, as indicated by Sir John Anderson[11] in the House of Commons, are based on my Report and accord largely with my Report . . . The main difference of principle lies in rejection by the Government of the fourth of the fundamental principles of my Report, namely, adequacy of benefit in amount and in time. In my Report it is stated that 'the rates of benefit or pensions provided by Social Insurance should be such as to secure for all normal cases an income adequate for subsistence'. In accordance with this, the rates suggested are based on a study of the cost of subsistence. On the assumption of a level of prices about 25 per cent above that of 1938, 40/- [£2] a week is proposed as the joint benefit or pension for man and wife together, and 8/- [40p] a week, in addition to an assumed 1/- [5p] a week in kind, is proposed as the average cash allowance for a dependent child. The full rate of pension, however, is to be paid not at once but only at the end of a transition period. For this, a length of twenty years is suggested. During those twenty years the actual rate of joint pension will rise gradually from 25/- [£1.25] to the full 40/- [£2].

Sir John Anderson, on behalf of the Government, rejected the principle of relating rates of benefit to subsistence . . . He [also] rejected the proposal for a rising scale of pensions in favour of 'a definite rate of pension and a definite contribution, even if that initial rate is somewhat higher than that recommended under the Beveridge scheme'. No indication was given by any Government speaker of the 'definite rate' of pensions contemplated. But, in view of the terms of Sir John Anderson's announcement and of the emphasis laid by the Chancellor of the Exchequer upon the necessity for avoiding heavy expenditure immediately after the war, it hardly seems possible that a rate . . . of 40/- [£2] is contemplated for a joint pension.

The ground for the Government's rejection of my pensions plan is apparently the fear of incurring excessive commitments for pensions. 'Once contributions and benefits are fixed,' said Sir John Anderson,

95

'a very heavy commitment running into many hundreds if not thousands of millions of pounds would be immediately entered into.' That, however, applies to the Government's own proposals as much as to mine. It is true that under my proposals the cost of insurance pensions rises from £126 million in the first year of the scheme to £300 million after twenty years; but only part of this is due to increase in the rate of pensions. Part is due to the increase in the numbers of people of pensionable age, while another part is due to bringing in for pensions persons now excluded; the acceptance by the Government of my principle of comprehensiveness means that at some time or other during the twenty years all the excluded classes must receive pensions at the Government's 'definite rate' above my initial rate. Without an actuarial study (for which I have no material) it is not possible to state precisely how much of the rising cost of pensions is due to these two factors, of increased proportion of old people and an inclusion of new classes. It can, however, hardly be less than two-fifths the total increase of £174 million; that is to say, only three-fifths of that increase is due to making the pensions rise from their original 25/- [£1.25] to their ultimate 40/- [£2]. If, moreover, as proposed by the Government, the original rate is more than 25/- [£1.25], the difference between the cost in 1965 of their proposals and of my proposals is narrowed.

The difference of principle between the Government proposals and my Plan for Social Security comes to a head in their treatment of pensions. It is involved also in their proposals for children's allowances and for unemployment and disability benefit. At the assumed level of postwar prices the average subsistence cost per child, apart from rent, cannot be put below 9/- [45p]; the Government propose 5/- [25p] in cash plus 2/6 [12p] in kind, or 7/6 [37p] altogether; this is a gap which must be filled somehow in fixing scales of benefit, if these scales are to secure the minimum for subsistence. In regard to unemployment and disability benefit, the difference is not in rates but in duration; the Government hold that each of these benefits must be limited in time. This means that those whose sickness continues after that time will be reduced to pension level; those whose unemployment continues will presumably receive unemployment assistance subject to a means test. These proposals can be supported by administrative arguments. For the pensions proposal there is no argument save financial.

I am concerned, not with the immediate rate of pension but with the ultimate rate of pension at which we should aim. I suggest that our aim should be that every British citizen, who works while he can and contributes while he is working and earning, should be assured of an old age without want, without dependence on the young, and without the need for charity or assistance. The Government quite definitely reject this aim. Thirty-five shillings [£1.75] a week for a man and wife is not, on any reasonable forecast of the cost of living after this war, a 'reasonable insurance against want' – those are the words of the White Paper – unless by reasonable you mean inadequate.

Why do the Government reject this aim of adequate provision for old age? They give two reasons. The first is the great variety of individual needs. Of course, individual needs are very varied, just as the size of the feet of human beings are varied, but I do not think that the variety of human needs is a reason for deliberately aiming at something well below the average. It really is as though the President of the Board of Trade, on the grounds of the variety of people's feet, ordered the production of utility shoes two inches shorter than the average length. I suggest that the variety of individual needs is no reason for making your aim definitely well below what are likely to be the needs of the great mass of the people.

The second is a somewhat stronger reason, which may have moved the government more. It is the need for financial prudence referred to in Paragraph 86 of the White Paper. It is 'the compelling need for caution' which the Minister without Portfolio yesterday deduced from the fact that in 1975, the cost of the pensions will be £324,000,000. Why will the cost be so much? Because the old will be there and will need to be fed, and the real difference of cost between providing for them adequately by a subsistence pension and providing for them by inadequate pensions eked out by assistance on a means test is very small indeed. I do not know whether Hon. Members realize how small it is, but the difference between the cost of pensions, including assistance in the Government proposals and in the Report, is, in 1965, £15,000,000. For 1975, 30 years from now, the difference is not so easy to calculate exactly, but I estimate roughly that if the ultimate retirement pensions are made 40s [£2] a week in place of 35s [£1.75] a week, the pensions themselves in 1975 will cost about £50,000,000 more, while on the other hand, assistance would cost £25,000,000 or £30,000,000 less.

So all that is in question is £20,000,000 or £25,000,000, 30 years hence, when the national income may well be £8,000,000,000 or £9,000,000,000. For the sake of that the Government are proposing a scheme which does not enable the young people of this country to contribute for adequate pensions. Are we really going to say that this country is going to be so poor after this war that we cannot keep our old above want? Being above want does not mean relief on a means test. There is no greater discouragement to thrift than the prospect of being subject to a means test in old age. I urge that the Government should introduce a scheme by which all contribute for adequate pensions now. That will lower general taxation now and hardly increase it later. Prudence means providence and providence means making a provision for the aged and making that provision now and co-operatively . . .

May I say to you one word shortly on the question of the relation of benefit to price levels. I do not want, and I do not suppose any Member in the House wants, pensions and benefits on a sliding scale changing continually with the cost of living. The real reason we do not want it is that we do not want the cost of living to be changing continually. We cannot build up a good economic system when such changes are continually taking place. At the same time to have fixed benefits in money and to let prices rise indefinitely would be to cheat all expectations. I suggest that what we have to do about the cost of living is to make the very best possible estimate of where it will be possible to fix the general level of prices, and to keep to that general level of prices – I speak only of the general level of the cost of living after the war – and relate the benefits to it. I am sure that for other reasons the country will need to work out a policy of stabilizing the cost of living. With the present trends I think we have to contemplate more than a 25 per cent rise in prices after this war. My own view is that we may have to contemplate a rise of at least one-third. That, of course, would involve increasing all the money rates of benefit and contribution, but it would not increase the real cost in relation to the total national income, because salaries and wages as measured in money would have risen proportionately. We must make our estimate of where it is going to be possible to stabilize the cost of living after the war and relate the benefits to it, and afterwards have a policy for keeping the cost of living there.

3F 'Lower contributions', rearranging the Burden of a Flat Rate Scheme

Source: Why I am a Liberal (1945), pp. 99–104

(This extract reprints material which originally appeared as an article in *The Times* in January 1945.)

There are three points at which the scheme of contributions for social insurance proposed by the Government in their recent White Papers appears to call for reconsideration. These relate to the number of weekly contributions in each year assumed in determining the weekly rate of contribution; the division of the total contribution for industrial injury between the three parties – employee, employer and the State; and the contributions to be paid by those who have no employers.

The rate of weekly contribution required depends on an assumption as to the average number of contributions that will be made in the course of each year, after allowing for those weeks in which, through unemployment, disability, or other cause, no contribution is made. According to a written answer given to me by the Minister without Portfolio in the House on November 14, 1944, the rate of contribution proposed by the Government in Class I is reached by assuming that the average number of contributions in the course of each year will be 45.5 for men and 46 for women. This assumption depends in the main upon the amount of unemployment and of sickness allowed for in each year. It accepts presumably the percentage of unemployment of 8.5 allowed for in my original report and carried forward into the Government's new calculations, in spite of the fact that the Government have now announced a policy for maintaining a high and stable level of employment. In my original report I agreed with the Government Actuary that, as a measure of prudence, 8.5 per cent of unemployment should be allowed for, while pointing out that it should be possible to reduce unemployment below this level. In my unofficial report on full employment I put the rate to which unemployment can be reduced by suitable Government action at 3 per cent; this would reduce by nearly two-thirds the expenditure on unemployment and would increase at the same time the average number of weekly contributions made each year.

On the assumption of full employment the weekly rates of contribution proposed by the Government are materially too high. If unemployment is not more than 3 per cent, the proposed joint weekly contribution for men in Class I can be reduced by something like 1s 1d [5p] a week without increasing the burden on the State; this burden would indeed be lightened by savings on unemployment assistance. I suggest that the contribution of insured persons and their employers should be based on assuming 3 per cent of unemployment, and that the risk of failure to achieve the full employment, which is now accepted as a Government responsibility, should be borne by the State.

(Further reductions in employee contributions should be made because the *SIAS* allowance for sickness was also pessimistic and the State could pay one-third rather than one-sixth of the cost of industrial injury. The self-employed (Class II) contribution could be reduced if the cost of the 'missing employer's contribution' was not paid by the contributor as proposed in *SIAS*; this cost should be equally divided between the self-employed contributor and the State.)

Under all three heads I am suggesting changes which would reduce social insurance contributions either at the risk or at the expense of additional taxation. This is a recognition of the main scientific criticism that has been made of my proposals – namely, that the flat compulsory contributions involved are an undesirable form of taxation, because they take no account of capacity to pay; the employee's contribution is regressive taxation, forming a larger proportion of a small wage than of a large wage; the employer's contribution enters directly into costs of production. Several impartial critics have expressed a preference for the New Zealand system, under which the whole cost of social insurance is borne by a special income tax.

In my view, there are good reasons for retaining in British social insurance a substantial element of contribution, that is to say, of payments irrespective of capacity to pay. But it is not desirable to carry this principle of social insurance contribution too far. In so far as the suggestions made by me above would reduce the rate of weekly contribution while still leaving it substantial, they are, I believe, in accord with social and economic principle. The most important of them are based on the view that the State should carry the financial risk of failing to bring about the reduction of unemployment and of disease which is within its power, and is not within the power of insured persons and their employers.

4

Beveridge and Economic Theory: the Problem of Unemployment

If Beveridge is not honoured as an economist that is because in economics, as in most theoretical discourses, prestige is accorded to those figures, like Keynes, whose texts propose major reconceptualizations of the objects of the discourse. From this point of view, through his work on unemployment, Beveridge played an important secondary role as a promoter of the reconceptualizations which others had initiated. Three of his major texts, spread over 35 years, deal with the problem of unemployment. *Unemployment: a problem of industry*, published in 1909, was Beveridge's most important work of the Edwardian period. In 1930 this text was reissued in a new edition which reprinted the old text along with seven new chapters which analysed the phenomenon of persistent unemployment in the 1920s. Towards the end of the Second World War, *Full Employment in a Free Society* took an altogether fresh Keynesian look at the possibility of abolishing unemployment. In all three texts Beveridge accepted the premises and conclusions of the prevailing economic orthodoxy but, characteristically, he worked at the radical edge of this orthodoxy and as it changed so Beveridge modified his views about the nature and causes of unemployment. At the same time, the three texts on unemployment offer much more than a fluent up-to-date commentary on changing economic doctrines. In all these texts, Beveridge tries to find a space for the operation of new policy instruments which could curb unemployment but he seeks to do so without upsetting either economic theory or the real economy. Although this task defeated him in 1930, in their very different ways both the 1909 and 1944 texts were full of practical suggestions for a better (liberal) world. Beveridge's real inventiveness as an economist was manifest in his proposals for new policy instruments. If economists now show so little interest in evaluating these proposals, that is because their discourse has become a scholastic way of understanding the world rather than a practical way of changing it. To his credit, Beveridge held a different concept of the discourse.

When Beveridge published his 1909 text orthodox economics denied and ignored the problem of unemployment. (See, for example, Winch, 1969.) It was assumed that supply and demand for labour were brought together at an equilibrium price (or wage); labour was just like every other commodity sold in a market that cleared. On this view, involuntary unemployment, except of the most transient kind, was impossible. Thus the economics texts of the time scarcely mention the subject; even in the 1920 edition, there is only one index reference to unemployment in Marshall's *Principles*. But, despite this self-denying ordinance, unemployment would not go away. The economic depression of the mid-1880s led to the so-called 'discovery of unemployment'. The political events of that time – especially the 1886 clashes in Hyde Park and Trafalgar Square and the 1889 dock strike – provoked a reconceptualization of the problem. As Stedman Jones (1971) has argued, the old mid-Victorian concern with pauperization and demoralization was replaced with a new concern about urban degeneration. Within this framework, social investigators like Booth and Rowntree organized new kinds of investigation into casual labour and urban poverty which provided evidence on problems of irregular work and low wages. By the 1900s, the economists were being outflanked by a new breed of freelance social investigators who defined unemployment as a social problem in a policy-oriented discourse. Beveridge's mission of 1909 was to attempt a reconciliation; without denying the results of social investigation, he would reclaim unemployment as a distinctively economic problem and do so in a way which did not threaten the central tenets of orthodox economics.

The trick was worked by the way in which the main causes of unemployment were analysed in the 1909 text. As extract 4A1 shows, Beveridge started from the orthodox premise that a general imbalance between the supply and demand for labour was impossible. *Unemployment* explicitly rejected the radical economic theory of J. A. Hobson who, in *The Physiology of Industry* (1896), had argued that the capitalist system had an inherent tendency towards underconsumption or oversaving. In Beveridge's text, Hobson suffered the indignities usually reserved for dissident intellectuals; Hobson's position was not only rejected, it was also grossly misrepresented because Hobson was presented as a theorist who was opposed to saving and advocated completely equal distribution of income as the only remedy for underconsumption (extract 4A3). With Hobson cleared out of the way, Beveridge could safely attribute unemployment to a variety of causes other than underconsumption. As extract 4A1 shows, Beveridge attributed unemployment to three causes:

(1) 'transformation of industrial structure', or structural change by which 'specific trades' decayed or changed production methods and shed labour;
(2) periodic 'fluctuations of economic activity', or seasonal and cyclical fluctuations in economic activity as a result of which labour demand in any trade varied over time;
(3) 'reserves of labour', or the tendency of industries to hold a frictional reserve stock of workers wherever the demand for labour was 'dissipated between many centres of employment'.

Since Beveridge wanted to maintain an orthodox position on the impossibility of general oversupply, cyclical fluctuations were a problem; he was forced to admit that they provided 'an object lesson of what might be expected if the supply of labour should ever come permanently to outstrip the demand' (extract 4A1). But Beveridge got round the awkward corner in two ways: first, he argued that cyclical fluctuations were, like structural change, necessary to the progress of a market system which provided 'the means by which the standard of production and of comfort is driven upwards' (extract 4A3); and second, he flatly asserted that 'reserve of labour' was 'apparently far more important' as a cause of unemployment.

In 1909, Beveridge's intellectual strategy was to represent as much unemployment as possible as a frictional problem. The 'conditions of employment' became the key to understanding and remedying the problem.

The normal state of every industry is to be overcrowded with labour, in the sense of having drawn into it more men than can ever find employment in it at the same time. This is the direct consequence of the work of each industry being distributed between many separate employers each subject to fluctuations of fortune. It depends upon the nature of the demand for labour, not upon the volume of the whole supply. (extract 4A2)

If this position was determined by Beveridge's desire to maintain economic orthodoxy, it did take Beveridge to a kind of limit position in that discourse. When so much emphasis was placed on friction, Beveridge had to deny the standard economic concept of labour as a kind of undifferentiated homogeneous commodity.

The demand for labour has been taken for purposes of argument as if it were single and concentrated; the supply of labour as if it were infinitely mobile and adaptable. The demand is, in fact, broken up by distinctions of price and quality, and subject to perpetual change and fluctuation. (extract 4B3)

If the labour market was not working as economic theory supposed, Beveridge's ideologically resourceful solution was to reform the labour market rather than rethink economic theory. When it came to new policy instruments, Beveridge proposed 'a policy of making reality correspond with the assumptions of economic theory' (extract 4B3).

In the Marxist concept of the 'reserve army of labour', the reserve was seen as a necessary and irremediable feature of capitalism. In Beveridge's concept of the 'reserve of labour' it was argued that the size of the reserve could be very much reduced to an 'irreducible minimum' through improvements in industrial organization. Labour exchanges and unemployment insurance became the key policy instruments because they could promote an 'organized and informed fluidity of labour'. Labour exchanges would immediately and constantly bring together all those looking for work with employers who had work to offer; all the particular variations in supply and demand would be matched as far as possible. It was envisaged that labour exchanges would have a monopoly of hiring and there would be compulsory notification of vacancies; Beveridge insisted that employers should send to exchanges 'for every man they require, and take no man through other avenues at all' (extract 4B1). After this 'organization of the labour market' had abolished unnecessary frictional unemployment, some unemployment attributable to other causes would still persist. Beveridge therefore proposed unemployment insurance as a second major policy instrument. Contributory unemployment insurance would provide limited income maintenance for those who were temporarily unemployed; as Beveridge explained, unemployment insurance offered 'for the individual workman an averaging of earnings between good and bad times' (extract 4B2). The two major policy instruments neatly complemented each other; insurance would help maintain those whose search for work was not immediately satisfied via the exchanges which provided a new safeguard against malingering because the genuineness of unemployment could always be tested with the offer of a job. Behind the two complementary major instruments of exchanges and insurance was the corollary policy of poor law reform. Through a policy of 'decasualization', the exchanges would, in effect, concentrate the available employment and provide regular work for that group of the unemployed who needed only work; a residuum of the unemployable would be 'sifted out' and consigned to a reformed poor law which would offer graded treatment including the option of disciplinary 'penal colonies'.

If the objective was to make reality correspond with economic theory, the great weakness of the 1909 text was that its prescriptions were not rested on a serious empirical analysis of the reality of the labour market; that task was taken up for the first time in 1911 by Rowntree and Lasker. When Beveridge wrote in 1909, he had no evidence on the local or national importance of different kinds of unemployment; crucially, his text contained no measurement of the size of the frictional 'reserve' and of the extent of the gap between the reserve and the 'irreducible minimum'. More generally, labour exchanges only offered sizeable benefits if existing patterns of working-class job search were inefficient; Beveridge never established that the working class did usually obtain jobs through that system of random searching which he described as the 'hawking of labour'. The whole policy solution of 1909 was a daring (or foolhardy) gambit which mainly satisfied the requirements of the theoretical predefinition of the problem in economics. If Beveridge's reputation survived and grew after 1909, that was because his policy instruments were either not implemented or implemented in circumstances which did not constitute a serious test of their appropriateness. Labour exchanges were introduced in 1909, but with voluntary notification of vacancies so that they could never be used for the organization of the labour market which Beveridge had envisaged; exchanges helped employers and employees fill up to one-third of all vacancies in the 1920s but, in Beveridge terms, they coerced nobody because irregular casual work continued and no unemployables were 'sifted out' into penal colonies. As for unemployment insurance, that was not tested because, in the period immediately after 1911, the scheme operated in good times and, in the interwar period after 1921, the principle of contributory insurance was overwhelmed by mass unemployment. All this Beveridge turned to his advantage because in his new text of 1930 he could argue that unemployment remained a problem partly because the policies of 1909 'have not been carried through' (extract 4C1).

The relevance of the old remedies could be and was reasserted in 1930 when Beveridge concluded that 'effective organization of the labour market is even more needed today than it seemed to be twenty years ago' (extract 4C1). This point was underscored by Beveridge's decision to reprint the complete text of the 1909 book as the first half of the 1930 book. But, at the same time, Beveridge had to recognize that the interwar unemployment problem was different and required a different analysis, which the second half of the 1930 book did supply. In the 1920s, as in the 1930s, the number of unemployed workers never dropped below one million and, in percentage terms, that meant more than 10 per cent of the workforce was unemployed. It was difficult to make comparisons with the pre-1914 period because the trade union unemployment statistics of that era never measured general unemployment. But it was plausible to suppose that by 1930 Britain had experienced almost a complete decade of continuous mass unemployment at a level and on a scale which was unknown before 1914. In the mid-1920s, it had been possible to attribute much of this unemployment to postwar problems of structural adjustment especially in the old export staple trades of coal, cotton, iron and steel and shipbuilding. Although such industries continued to account for a significant proportion of unemployment, by 1930 Beveridge, like most contemporaries, found the structural explanation was inadequate. As he pointed out 'the war is now more than ten years behind us' (extract 4C3). In the Midlands and the south of Britain there were expanding industries and districts with lower unemployment rates. But the process of structural adjustment had somehow failed because, even at the growth points, there were no industries or districts with unemployment as low as or lower than before the war (extract 4C3). There had been a general and sustained rise in the level of unemployment.

In analysing this new phenomenon, Beveridge in 1930 simply borrowed the orthodox classical explanation which was then offered by economists like Pigou. If mass unemployment persisted and the labour market did not clear, that must be because wages were too high. More exactly,

> the widespread enduring unemployment that we find in Great Britain is just what we should expect to find as the result of an abnormal rise of wages, unaccompanied by an equal rise of productivity or cheapening of capital. (extract 4C3)

The implication was that, if real wages were to fall, then unemployment would vanish like snow in May. In a second stage of the analysis, it was therefore necessary to specify why wages were rigid and sticky. In a way that was becoming familiar, Beveridge identified 'two new factors [which] had come in to make money wages less plastic downwards' than they had been before 1914; the first of these factors preventing natural adjustment was the growth of unionism and the spread of collective bargaining and the second factor was the introduction of the dole for the unemployed.

The classical explanation of unemployment is still with us; if the dates and figures were changed Beveridge's account could be published in the 1980s as right-wing, anti-Keynesian economic journalism. The obvious and immediate question is whether this explanation was (and is) true. But this turns out to be a *question mal posée* which cannot be directly answered because theoretical explanations cannot be easily refuted within the circle of their own assumptions and supporting evidence. For those who accept the laws of supply and demand and the marginal product theory of wages, the classical explanation must be true. Thus, for example, Beveridge in 1930 argued that it was a matter of elementary economic theory that if unemployment persisted 'demand for and supply of labour are not finding their appropriate price for meeting' (extract 4C3). Furthermore, those who accept the classical framework can usually find empirical evidence which corroborates their explanation. In 1930 Beveridge's central exhibit was a graph (Figure 4.1) which showed an 'uncanny' parallel movement of the curve of real wages and unemployment rates; on this basis Beveridge concluded 'it hardly seems reasonable . . . to doubt the connection' (extract 4C3). And yet, after fifty years of rehearsal, this kind of evidence and argument never convinces sceptics who doubt the framework.

The crucial point is that, even if the classical explanation is true, it is irrelevant because none of its protagonists can specify the policy instruments which will secure the necessary reduction in wages. It is significant that the task of specifying appropriate policy instruments was beyond Beveridge who had a genius for specifying new policy instruments. Although Beveridge attributed wage rigidity to unionism and the dole, in 1930 he could make no suggestions for modifying these institutional conditions. He could not countenance any withdrawal of the dole; he did believe in the reassertion of the contributory principle which would re-establish time limits on insurance benefit but, in labour market terms, that would not change anything because he proposed indefinite means-tested relief allowances for those who exhausted insurance benefit (extract 4C3). As for an attack on unionism, that possibility was never discussed because Beveridge in 1930 believed that trade unions were politically desirable and knew that, in the aftermath of the 1926 General Strike, an attack on unionism was not politically feasible. When a direct attack on institutional rigidities is ruled out, then, as extract 4C4 shows, Beveridge's discussion of what is to be done inevitably tails off in an inconclusive way. Beveridge argued that a negative policy of lowering wages was in any case economically undesirable because it reduced the incentives to efficiency. The only option therefore is a positive policy of raising productivity which naturally increases very slowly. But Beveridge is coy about how the required increase in productivity could be obtained; whether and how it can be brought about 'must be left for discussion elsewhere and by others' (extract 4C4). In the mean time, Beveridge can only urge union leaders to make responsible wage claims and regret the selfishness of those in employment who defend their living standards through wage settlements which ensure someone else's unemployment. When nothing can be done about unemployment, classical economists in the 1930s (or the 1980s) can only insist that we must all accept our share of the blame.

In 1930 Beveridge set the problem of unemployment in a classical framework and supposed that it could only be tackled at the micro level in the labour market. Despite his failure to specify instruments adequate to this task, in 1930 other policies, such as tariffs or public works, were regarded as more or less irrelevant. Thus *Unemployment* (1930) took what was then the orthodox economic line on public works, In principle, public works could reduce unemployment but in practice they could not be used to eliminate mass unemployment; Beveridge argued that public works had a limited role in providing jobs for older immobile workers in depressed mining areas (*Unemployment*, 1930, pp. 143–5). The 1944 report on *Full Employment* confronts the same elementary facts as the 1930 text; 'an unplanned market economy is less automatically self-adjusting at a high level of employment than had been supposed in earlier times' (extract 4D1). But the 1944 report exuded confidence and attack in contrast to the disappointment and defence of the 1930 text. The change of tone is possible because by 1944 Beveridge is posing the problem of unemployment in a new Keynesian framework and arguing for its solution at a newly identified macroeconomic level.

In 1944, unemployment is attributed to deficiency of aggregate demand.

The revolution of economic thought effected by J. M. Keynes, aided by the experience of the thirties, lies in the fact that adequate demand for labour is no longer taken for granted. The Keynesian analysis leads to the conclusion that, even apart from cyclical depression, there may be chronic or nearly chronic deficiency in the total demand for labour, with full employment a rare fleeting accident. (extract 4D1)

This conception did represent a real break with classical theory but, if the Keynesian revolution was successful, this was partly because, through various intellectual sleights of hand, Keynes was able to (mis)represent his *General Theory* of 1936 as a complement or supplement to classical theory (see Cutler *et al.*, 1986). By this means underconsumption and underinvestment were admitted into an orthodox economics which had hitherto denied their possibility; the *General Theory* may have been published by Macmillan but it quickly acquired the imprimatur of Cambridge. In this context, Beveridge, who had resisted the Hobsonian heresy of oversaving, accepted the new Keynesian orthodoxy of underconsumption and underinvestment. Like most intellectuals writing after a theoretical revolution, in 1944 Beveridge rewrote the history of his own development so that his earlier work became pre-Keynesian rather than anti-Keynesian. It was asserted that his 1909 text and the 1936 *General Theory* represented 'complementary' approaches to the problem of unemployment. Beveridge in 1944 admitted that his first study had assumed 'demand would look after itself' but argued (quite falsely) that 'my first study did not deny the possibility of deficiency in total demand' (extract 4D1).

Beveridge in 1944 enlisted on the Keynesian side that was winning, but at this stage the Keynesian victory was not complete. The *General Theory* had reconceptualized the causes of unemployment but had not specified the policy instruments which could abolish the unemployment caused by 'chronic or recurrent deficiency of demand' (extract 4D1). Without such instruments the new Keynesian orthodoxy would be as irrelevant as the old classical orthodoxy. The Keynesian economic problem was recurrent deficiency of investment expenditure whenever business expectations were pessimistic; consumption expenditure could not normally compensate because the marginal propensity to consume was below one. In the *General Theory* of 1936 the main policy emphasis fell on a proposal for the 'socialization of investment' whereby counter-cyclical investment funds would be mobilized by the state and allocated according to non-market criteria. Intervention of this kind was technically difficult and politically problematic for liberal collectivists who favoured a limited intervention which left market freedom intact. In his important 1940 pamphlet, *How To Pay for the War*, Keynes shifted the focus of attention on to the consumption expenditure component of aggregate demand; Keynes was then particularly exercised by the problem of curbing wartime excess demand, but his suggested fiscal instruments could easily be adapted to deal with demand deficiency in a postwar depression. At this stage, Beveridge joined the Keynesians and took up the task of developing new policy instruments.

Beveridge never relinquished the old policy instruments of 1909; when the labour market had never been 'organized', he claimed the old policy instruments were as relevant as when originally proposed thirty-five years previously. But the old instruments could hardly be strategically important when Beveridge was working in a new framework where demand deficiency was represented as the cause or precondition of most frictional and structural unemployment (extract D1). The crucial issue was how to tackle demand deficiency. And Beveridge's answer was by indirect means, through the instrument of a new kind of fiscal policy which embodied 'the principle of budgeting for full employment' (extract 4E2). The old Gladstonian rules of sound finance should be rejected; there was no virtue in balancing the budget or reducing state expenditure to a minimum (see Middleton, 1985). The new first rule of Beveridge's Keynesianism was 'total outlay at all times must be sufficient for full employment' (extract 4E2) and the state should tax and borrow, even to the extent of incurring budget deficits, with the aim of ensuring consumption and investment demand sufficient to employ the whole workforce.

Beveridge's solution of the 1940s is different from that of the Keynesianism of the 1950s which relied on fiscal manipulation of income tax, purchase tax and hire purchase regulations to adjust private consumption expenditure. Like this later kind of Keynesianism, Beveridge believed in taxing for full employment rather than borrowing for full employment; Beveridge explicitly rejected the latter option because it would increase the size and power of a capitalist rentier class (extract 4E2). But Beveridge wanted to do more than trim private consumption to maintain permanent full employment;

> some redistribution of private incomes, increasing the propensity to consume, should be part of a full employment policy. But it cannot be the whole of that policy or its main instrument. (extract 4E2)

He envisaged that taxation would be used 'as a means of reducing private expenditure on consumption and thereby freeing real resources for other uses' (extract 4E2). Optimistically he believed that, for twenty years after the war, 'definite common objectives' would lead 'the good sense of the community' to accept higher public expenditure, to prefer 'planned outlay . . . to unplanned outlay' (extract 4E2). For the foreseeable future, social priorities, and especially investment in homes, schools and hospitals, should have priority. Beveridge in 1944 wrote the charter for the postwar austerity years under Labour, he did not license the subsequent Tory boom.

The 1944 report is the most radical of Beveridge's texts because it presupposes that social priorities will be imposed in many spheres of economic and social life. This is reflected in the way in which Beveridge presents full employment as a means rather than an end.

> The object of all human activity is not employment but welfare, to raise the material standard of living and make opportunities for wider spiritual

life. For these purposes the wise direction of outlay and so of employment, in the general interest of the community, is only less important than the adequacy of outlay as a whole. (extract 4E2)

But it should be noted that Beveridge did not recommend socialism, because social priorities would only be imposed in a liberal collectivist way up to a minimum beyond which individual responsibility would reign.

In the total outlay directed to maintain full employment, priority is required for a minimum for all citizens of housing, health, education and nutrition, and a minimum of investment to raise the standard of life of future generations. The democratic state must be guided, and can safely be guided by social priorities up to that minimum. (extract 4E2)

This position, however, is ambiguous because Beveridge extends the concept of the minimum beyond the 'income subsistence' of *SIAS* without specifying what would constitute a minimum in areas like health, housing and education.

On the central issue of full employment the 1944 report is confident and optimistic. Beveridge believed that unemployment, which had averaged over 10 per cent in the interwar period, could be reduced to 3 per cent or less. Indeed he defined full employment as a state in which the demand for labour 'always' exceeded the supply so that 'jobs, rather than men, should wait' (extract 4E1). In this situation all the unemployment that remained would be of a short-run frictional kind. If he was optimistic about the level of employment which could be maintained, like others who operated in a Keynesian problematic, Beveridge assumed that the composition of employment would not be a problem. Issues about gender and skill requirements were simply not discussed in the 1944 report. Beveridge's expectation of a low participation rate for married women was consonant with prewar experience (*Full Employment*, 1944, pp. 369–70); but the prediction that the vast majority of married women would make 'marriage their sole occupation' rested more on his own hopes and prejudices than on social observation. As for the male occupied population, it was simply assumed that a high level of demand would suppress problems arising from the composition of demand for labour; full employment meant the availability of 'jobs at fair wages, of such a kind, and so located that the unemployed man can reasonably be expected to take them' (*Full Employment*, 1944, p. 18).

It was always doubtful whether the single instrument of budgetary policy was adequate or appropriate for dealing with problems about the composition of employment which have become more acute in the postwar period (see Cutler *et al.* 1986). Optimism about full employment was more justified because, unlike the classicals, the Keynesians had specified instruments which could influence the level of employment. But, as we now know, the problem of maintaining full employment had not been solved because the conditions of application of these instruments cannot be easily satisfied in an economy which is well away from full employment. The conclusion to this book develops our argument that Keynesian demand management policies cannot in practice be easily used to deliver full employment in such an economy. It should be noted that this problem did surface at one point in Beveridge's 1944 text, when he discussed the international preconditions for Keynesianism in one country. Beveridge accepted that full employment was not a matter of independent domestic decision for Britain. As extract 4E4 shows, he recognized that mass unemployment could only be avoided if all the ir.dustrial countries committed themselves to the maintenance of full employment and did so in a payments system where successful countries with payments surpluses recycled this purchasing power in the form of long-term loans to the less fortunate. In the 1980s, it is obvious that these conditions cannot be easily satisfied.

In 1909 Beveridge presented unemployment as a problem which could be solved through the exercise of the will:

> There is something almost fantastic in supposing that a nation capable of raising the efficiency of British industry must be forever baffled by the business problem of organizing and maintaining adequately the reserve forces of labour. The question is simply that of determining that the problem shall be solved. (*Unemployment*, 1909, p. viii)

His own work shows how and why the problem is more intractable; unemployment can be curbed only if the problem is reconceptualized so that points of intervention are discovered and if practically applicable policy instruments are specified. Beveridge's work on economics is still of importance because it highlights these issues.

4A The Problem Definition of 1909: 'A Problem of Industrial Organization'

Source: *Unemployment: a problem of industry* (1909)

A1 *The Three Main Causes of Unemployment (p. 12)*

While the final absorption of the growing population in growing industry is accepted as being for this country still happily the rule, it is no less necessary to admit the existence of facts modifying the completeness of this absorption at certain times and places – indeed, at all times and places. There is no general want of adjustment between the natural increase of the people and the expansion of industry, between the rate of supply of fresh labour and the normal growth of the demand for it. There are specific imperfections of adjustment which are the economic causes of unemployment.

One of these has long been recognized. While industry, as a whole, grows, specific trades may decay, or change in methods and organization. The men who have learnt to live by those trades may find their peculiar and hard-won skill a drug on the market and themselves permanently displaced from their chosen occupations, while lacking both the youth and the knowledge to make their way into new occupations . . .

A second type of maladjustment between the demand for and the supply of labour is found in actual fluctuations of industrial activity. Many trades, perhaps most trades, pass regularly each year through an alternation of busy and slack seasons, determined by climate or social habits, or a combination of both. Building is slack in winter and busy in spring and summer. Printers find least to do in the August holidays and most in the season just before Christmas. At the London Docks timber comes in at one time of the year; fruit at another; tea at a third. Behind and apart from these seasonal vicissitudes of special trades, and affecting, though in varying degrees, nearly all trades at about the same time, is a cyclical fluctuation in which periods of general depression – 1868, 1879, 1885–6, 1893–5, 1904 – alternate at irregular intervals with periods of feverish activity – 1872–4, 1881, 1889–90, 1899–1900. At such times of depression the industrial system does appear to suffer a temporary loss of elasticity; it fails for a while to keep pace with the steady growth of the population; it gives – in a phase of falling wages and lowered standards – an object lesson of what might be expected if the supply of labour should ever come permanently to outstrip the demand.

These two elements in the problem of unemployment have long been familiar. A third, apparently far more important than either the occasional transformations of industrial structure or the periodic fluctuations of industrial activity, is only just beginning to receive attention. This is the requirement in each trade of reserves of labour to meet the fluctuations of work incidental even to years of prosperity. The men forming these reserves are constantly passing into and out of employment. They tend, moreover, to be always more numerous than can find employment together at any one time. This tendency springs directly from one of the fundamental facts of industry – the dissipation of the demand for labour in each trade between many separate employers and centres of employment. Its result may be described as the normal glutting of the labour market. The counterpart of such glutting is the idleness at every moment of some or others of those engaged.

A2   *The Reserve of Labour (pp. 70, 77, 99–100, 103)*

The condition of the labour market appears to present a standing contradiction of economic laws. Whatever the demand for labour, the supply tends always and everywhere, not to coincide with it, but to exceed it.

This is the central paradox of the unemployed problem. Why should it be the normal condition of the labour market to have more sellers than buyers, two men to every job and not at least as often two jobs to every man? The explanation of the paradox is really a very simple one – that there is no one labour market but only an infinite number of separate labour markets . . .

There is, in truth, no such thing as the demand of an industry for labour, except as an arithmetical abstraction. The actual demand is that of each of many separate employers in many different places. Because of this separation the actual aggregate force of these demands is normally in excess of the arithmetical aggregate; opposite variations are not set off against one another in practice as they are in the statistics. The actual supply tends of course to conform to the actual demand; that is to say, it tends normally to be in excess of the arithmetical aggregate of the separate demands. In other words, the normal state of every industry is to be overcrowded with labour, in the sense of having drawn into it more men than can ever find employment in it at the same time. This is the direct consequence of the work of each industry being distributed between many separate employers each subject to fluctuations of fortune. It depends upon the nature of the demand for labour, not upon the volume of the whole supply. It is the simple explanation of the irreducible minimum of unemployment shown by the trade union returns.

The widening of the discussion from the irreducible minimum of unemployment to the reserve of labour is necessary because the individuals who at any moment constitute the minimum are an indistinguishable part of a much larger body of men subject to irregularity of employment, subject, that is, to constant leakage of earning power. The special significance of the irreducible minimum of unemployment is merely this: that in nearly every industry the fringe of irregular workmen is greater in fact than is arithmetically necessary. It is never all needed at once; some part is always standing idle. The actual leakage of labour power through irregularity of employment is more than that involved in the fluctuation of the industry as a whole. The number of men drawn into a trade by the scattered demand of a multiplicity of employers is normally in excess of what would be the maximum requirements of the trade, if its activity – remaining unchanged in amount and fluctuation – were concentrated at one place in the hands of a single firm. In other words, the irreducible minimum of unemployment in any trade indicates the degree of friction in the movement of labour. It represents that proportion of the total reserve which might be dispensed with if the labour market in the trade, instead of being broken up into many markets, were unified and organized.

A3   The Nature of Cyclical Fluctuations (pp. 62–4)

There is some reason for saying that cyclical fluctuation of trade depends directly upon the abundance of capital available for new enterprises and upon industrial competition; that it represents, in fact, the incessantly renewed attempt and partial failure to put into operation productive forces normally in excess of the existing demand. There is no justification for a practical inference from this that an attempt should be made to prevent cyclical fluctuation by destroying competition or drying up the springs of capital . . . Mr

Hobson,[1] no doubt, would reply that his attack is not upon saving but oversaving, and that he quite recognizes the need of some provision for future production. His point is simply that this provision is now excessive because saving is too easy; his remedy is to make saving harder. In just the same spirit, Mr Bradlaugh and Mrs Besant,[2] thirty years ago, would have explained that they were attacking, not all increase of the population, but only excessive increase. They started a movement, however, which shows no sign of regarding this nice distinction and yearly brings the nation into increasing alarm lest it cease to grow at all. So Mr Hobson, in making saving harder, can hold out no guarantee that he will not make it too hard and thus stop industrial progress altogether. If incomes were so far equalized that all saving meant sacrifice of a keenly desired present good for a future one, it is extremely likely that no sufficient provision for new capital would be made at all. There is, indeed, no possibility of determining *a priori* how the national dividend can best be allocated between immediate consumption and investment in the means of future production. In other words, there is no criterion for saying beforehand what is *over*saving and what is not. The right adjustment, however, comes about naturally through economic forces . . .

No doubt the adjustment takes time and may only be accomplished with a certain amount of friction and loss. The need for adjustment can, however, only be avoided by abolishing either the possibility of producing beyond existing demand, or the competitive stimulus to such production, that is to say, by abolishing either the possibility of, or the principal factor in, material progress.

Trade fluctuation is, indeed, at times obviously and directly the means by which the standard of production and of comfort is driven upwards. When trade is expanding many new factories are built; they have then their chance to overcome initial difficulties and to get a footing while competition is less severe. When trade contracts again it is not the new but the old and relatively obsolete factories that have to close. The next expansion starts from a higher level of efficiency. In this way fluctuation appears intimately bound up with the possibility of material progress. The recurrent failure to operate means of production ahead of the existing demand is only partial. Each wave leaves wages higher or prices lower and productivity greater than did the wave before.

No one theory as to the cause of trade fluctuation can yet be taken

117

as proved. All those mentioned must be treated at best as no more than hypotheses to be tested by the facts. It may well prove that no one of them will fit all the facts, just as it is certain that they are by no means mutually exclusive. Whatever, however, the explanation to be finally adopted, there seems now some reason in theory for regarding fluctuation as inevitable or at least as preventible only at the cost of greater harm.

A4 Character Defects and Volume of Unemployment (pp. 134–5)

There are, no doubt, a certain number of men who, though apparently able-bodied, form no part of the industrial world and do not wish to do so. They swell the volume of idleness in a country but hardly in a strict sense that of unemployment; they cannot appropriately be described as men out of work because they are never in work. They are the social parasites most prominently represented by the habitual criminal and the habitual vagrant. Each of these is in truth as definitely diseased as are the inmates of hospitals, asylums and infirmaries, and should be classed with them . . . There is a definite though small class of men always in and out of prison. There is a definite though not very large class of men always in and out of the workhouses, shelters, and casual wards. These are 'unemployable' in the full sense of the word . . .

If, therefore, certain degenerate human types could be abolished, and if the common level of human nature – in respect of assiduity, sobriety, adaptability and all the other virtues – could be raised, the volume of idleness, whether voluntary or involuntary, would no doubt be diminished. To this extent it is right to urge improvement of human character as a remedy for unemployment. The limitations on this admission have, however, to be carefully noted. First, the number of the entirely unemployable class, though uncertain, is certainly not very great. Second, the most practical way of improving human character lies often in abolishing industrial or social conditions which induce or pander to the vices of idleness, slovenliness and irresponsibility. Third, no conceivable improvement in the character of the workmen will eliminate the main economic factors in unemployment.

4B The 1909 Solution of 'Organization of the Labour Market'

Source: Unemployment: a problem of industry (1909)

B1 *The Organization of the Labour Market via Exchanges (pp. 198, 215)*

The deliberate organization of the labour market is the first step in the permanent solution of the problem of unemployment.

The organization of the labour market means simply that there shall be known centres or offices or exchanges, to which employers shall send or go when they want workpeople, to which workpeople shall go when they want employment. When for any trade this has been carried so far that all employers in it send to the same exchange or one of a series of connected exchanges for every man they require, and take no man through other avenues at all, then the labour market for that one trade may be said to be completely organized. When for any industrial district this has been carried so far that all the trades in it use the same exchange or all the separate trade exchanges are connected, then the labour market for that district may be said to be completely organized. When all over the United Kingdom and for every trade in it there is a connected system of labour exchanges so that no man thinks of applying anywhere else either for workpeople or employment and would not get either if he did, then the labour market for the United Kingdom may be said to be completely organized . . .

And last, an aspect of labour market organization has to be mentioned, lying perhaps a little apart from the present subject but of fundamental importance. This is the function of an efficient labour exchange in affording a direct test of unemployment. The central problem of the Poor Law is to relieve without relieving unnecessarily. The only principle on which it has hitherto attempted to secure this is the principle of deterrence – the making of relief so repellent that men might be presumed to have exhausted every other resource before they would accept it . . . To deterrence the labour exchange offers an alternative and a supplement. If all the jobs offering in a trade or a district are registered at a single office, then it is clear that any man who cannot get work through that office is unemployed against his will. He may be relieved without deterrence, yet without any fear that he is being relieved when he could get work, or is being drawn needlessly from industry to pauperism.

B2 Unemployment Insurance as a 'Second Line of Attack' (pp. 223, 226, 229)

[Even with exchanges some unemployment was unavoidable.]

There is needed . . . also some other method applicable both to general depression in trades where organized short time proves impossible and to all the incalculable varieties of individual misfortune. This, it is here suggested, is to be sought in some form of insurance against unemployment.

The term 'insurance' in this connection cannot be used as a term of art. It must be taken to apply loosely to any process whereby each of a number of workmen sets aside something of his wages while earning, in order to obtain an allowance in case of unemployment. It need not be taken as excluding the possibility of grants to the insurance fund from other sources. Its essence is for the individual workman an averaging of earnings between good and bad times, and for the body of workmen a sharing of the risks to which they are all alike exposed . . .

The method of insurance is flexible as no provision of relief by employment can be flexible. No temporary or accidental stoppage is too small for it. The machinery of assistance is always ready; so soon as a man becomes unemployed, from whatever cause, he has only to begin signing the vacant book in order to become entitled at once or in a few days to an allowance. On the other hand, the severest depression of trade is hardly too great to be dealt with in this way . . .

No scheme of insurance – or of any other honourable provision for unemployment – can be safe from abuse unless backed by an efficient organization of the labour market, i.e. by a fairly complete registration of all the employment offering. On the other hand, with that complete registration the insurance or relief fund has an absolute protection; the men if they too are compelled to register at the same office, cannot remain on the fund one moment after there is work anywhere available for them to do. Once the community or the insurance fund undertakes the notification of work the necessity of making relief allowances inadequate or degrading in order to drive men on the search for work disappears. The trade unions cannot safely now make their benefits really adequate simply because, though they have something of a registration system, they have very little; they still rely mainly upon their members finding work by personal application.

Insurance against unemployment, therefore, stands in the closest relation to the organization of the labour market, and forms the second line of attack on the problem of unemployment. It is, indeed, the necessary supplement thereto. The labour exchange is required to reduce to a minimum the intervals between successive jobs. Insurance is required to tide over the intervals that will still remain. The labour exchange mobilizes the reserves of labour for fluctuations and hastens reabsorption after changes of industrial structure. Insurance is needed to provide for the maintenance of the reserves while standing idle and of the displaced men while waiting for reabsorption.

B3 'Making Reality Correspond with the Assumptions of Economic Theory' (pp. 216, 231)

The object of labour market organization is the close, continuous and automatic adjustment of existing demand and supply over the largest possible area. The weakness alike of theory and practice in regard to unemployment in the past has been the assumption that this adjustment was already substantially secured; in other words, that the force of friction might be neglected. The demand for labour has been taken for purposes of argument as if it were single and concentrated; the supply of labour as if it were infinitely mobile and adaptable. The demand is, in fact, broken up by distinctions of place and quality, and subject to perpetual change and fluctuation. The supply is rendered immobile by ignorance and less adaptable by every year of age. Adam Smith and his followers were right in emphasizing the mobility of labour as a cardinal requirement of industry. The practical application of their teaching has been inadequate because it has been confined to abolishing visible and legal obstacles to motion, such as the laws of settlement and of apprenticeship. It has left untouched the impalpable but no less real barriers of ignorance, poverty and custom. If friction and the waste involved in friction are to be eliminated from the labour market, there must be, not mere absence of legal obstacles, but organized and informed fluidity of labour.

It is a policy of industrial organization; of meeting deliberately industrial needs that at present are met wastefully because without deliberation. Fluctuations of demand are now provided for by the maintenance of huge stagnant reserves of labour in varying extremities of distress. There is no reason in the nature of things why they should not be provided for by organized reserves of labour raised beyond the reach of distress. To be able to follow the demand men must possess greater powers of intelligent movement from place to place; they must possess also power to move from trade to trade, or – a more essential point – they must have better guidance in the first choice of occupations. To be able to wait for the demand men must have a reserve for emergencies; they must not be living from hand to mouth; they must through insurance or its equivalent be able to average wages over good and bad times and to subsist without demoralization till they can be reabsorbed again after industrial transformations. These two measures are complementary and, in some sense indeed, alternative to one another. The better the supply of labour is able to follow the demand, the less will it have to wait for the demand. The greater the power of waiting for the demand, that is to say, the higher the rate or the better the distribution of wages, the less need is there for movement . . .

It is a policy of making reality correspond with the assumptions of economic theory. Assuming the demand for labour to be single and the supply perfectly fluid, it is not hard to show that unemployment must always be in process of disappearance – that demand and supply are constantly tending to an equilibrium. The ideal for practical reform, therefore, must be to concentrate the demand and to give the right fluidity to the supply.

B4   The Residuum and a Reformed Poor Law (pp. 215, 233)

It may be asked; what the organization of the labour market would do for the unemployable. The answer is, that by regularizing employment it would sift them out of the industrial world altogether. Decasualization would gradually make it impossible to live by working two days a week and lying in bed for the rest, or by being 'weeded out' for incompetence on one building job after another. The work lost by these men – the unemployables on the fringe of industry – would go to make up a reasonable subsistence for others. These men would be left for disciplinary or hospital treatment under the Poor Law . . .

A reformed Poor Law . . . should be able to apply different measures to different cases. In respect of the able-bodied – to whom of course the discussion is here limited – three distinct forms of treatment are needed: provision of sustenance to keep men alive till they can recover employment; provision of restorative or educational treatment for those who are apparently not now fit to take employment even if it came their way; provision of disciplinary treatment subject to detention for those clearly beyond restoration by weaker measures, and perhaps beyond restoration by any measures at all. The present Poor Law, it will be seen, aims at meeting only the first of these three possible requirements of the able-bodied; it has in effect only one type of institution – whether called a workhouse, a casual ward or a stoneyard – where sustenance subject to deterrence is meted out to all and sundry. The reformed Poor Law must be prepared to meet all three requirements. It must have, first, the means of temporary assistance – something to correspond to the workhouses, casual words, stoneyards and relief works of today. This is for the 'unemployed'. It must have, second, the means of restoring to physical vigour and perhaps of training for new occupations those who are proved incapable of supporting themselves as they are – something corresponding or akin to the free farm colonies at Hollesley Bay[3] and elsewhere. This is for the 'unemployable' or 'half-employable' who can be restored. It must have, third, the means of separating from society those who are clearly unfit to belong thereto – something corresponding to the penal colonies in Belgium and Switzerland. This is for the 'unemployable' who perhaps cannot be made good again. Each of these three grades of treatment must be provided.

4C   The Impasse of 1930: Persistent Mass Unemployment with Sticky Wages

Source: Unemployment; a problem of industry, Part 2 (1930)

C1   *The policies of 1909 'Have Not Been Carried through' (pp. 401–3)*

Today the problem of unemployment bulks larger than ever. Was the old diagnosis wrong or is it out of date? Were the policies wrong or was their application mishandled?

A formal answer to these questions is that the continuance of unemployment cannot invalidate the diagnosis or the policies of 1909, because these policies have not been carried through. Unemployment insurance, with all its devices for reducing claims to benefit, has been transformed into unemployment relief. Labour Exchanges, after a hopeful start, were sunk in a flood of war tasks and postwar doles; they are now reviving as employment agencies; but their special and most needed service of decasualization has gone by the board . . .

Effective organization of the labour market is even more needed today than it seemed to be twenty years ago. New arguments have been added while the old ones remain, strengthened by new knowledge.

In the first place, in so far as unemployment today is due to permanent changes of industrial structure involving changes of location, rather than to transient depression, it is yet more important than before to make labour mobile, locally and between industries; it is yet less possible than before to leave men without guidance in the search for work . . .

All the old elements in the problem calling for labour market organization remain. The flux of employment – the ceaseless passing of men into and out of situations – persists; if not greater than it was before in fact, it is greater than most people would have thought possible. Seasonal employment persists with little or no formal dovetailing between them. The hawking of labour persists. Casual employment persists; the measure of this failure in twenty years to deal with 'the most potent, the most certain, and the most extensive in its operation . . . of all the causes or conditions predisposing to pauperism' is found in the 31 per cent of unemployment in dock and wharf labour, 23 per cent in works of construction, 13 per cent in building.

C2   What Is To Be Done with Unemployment Insurance? (pp. 406–9)

What judgement is to be passed on the . . . policy [of] unemployment insurance – or rather, what is to be done with the new form of relief to the able-bodied that has grown out of the insurance scheme of 1911?

The history of unemployment insurance is very different from that of labour market organization. In place of struggling for life against apathy and distrust, being thrust into a corner, being rejected wholly in the field of greatest service, as has been the fate of the Exchanges, insurance has grown to overshadow every other measure for dealing with unemployment. The first insurance scheme exacted a weekly contribution of 2.5*d* [1p] from each of less than 2.25 million workmen and added an equal contribution from their employer and about 1.66*d* from the State, in order to give the workman 7*s* [35p] a week for a maximum of fifteen weeks of unemployment in twelve months. The 2.25 million have become 12 million, the 5*d* [2p] from the employer and workman has become (for men) 15*d* [6p], the 7*s* [35p] a week has become 17*s* [85p], with substantial dependants' allowances in addition, the benefit has become practically unlimited in duration. The income of the unemployment fund, from an average of under 2.5 million pounds a year, has become 40 million.

With this growth of scale has come a fundamental change in the character of the scheme. It has been converted, practically since extended benefit became continuous in 1924, formally since standard benefit became unlimited on a flat rate of contributions in 1928, into a system of general unemployment relief financed mainly by a tax on employment. This has happened, under pressure of postwar conditions, because two of the main presuppositions of the insurance scheme were not fulfilled. The scheme of 1911 was meant to be accompanied both by effective organization of the labour market reducing industrial unemployment to its minimum, and by a reform of the Poor Law, giving appropriate relief in restorative institutions to those that fell through the meshes of insurance; it was never meant to be the last as well as the first defence against destitution.

The first step towards sound decision as to the future of the unemployment insurance scheme is to realize how completely its present differs from its past, and in the light of that realization to face frankly the alternative courses open and all that each involves – the alternative of getting back and going forward.

One alternative is to go further along the road already travelled, to recognize the seeming logic of events, and to regard every person as entitled to maintenance up to a certain level, irrespective of any contributions paid by him, so long as by signing regularly at a Labour Exchange he proves that he is genuinely unemployed – that is to say without work, able to work, and unable to get work.

This alternative dispenses with the need for any further agency, such as the Poor Law, for relief of the unemployed. It involves, however, reconsideration of the contributory system. Once the principle of insurance is abandoned for the principle of relief, the employer's and workman's contributions under the present scheme become a tax on employment with few compensating advantages; all the arguments urged in 1911 as to the advantage of interesting employers and workpeople in the solvency of the scheme and of making the workpeople see it as an extension of trade union benefits have disappeared. On fiscal grounds a tax on employment is hard to defend; it does not come out of profits; it goes directly into costs of production; it discourages a desirable activity. Admission of such a specialized tax throws away the main safeguard of economy in the British financial system – Treasury responsibility for the Budget; the tax is one likely to grow, as it has grown, rapidly. If unemployment insurance is going to become unemployment relief subject to the Labour Exchange test, the present plan of financing it mainly by a direct tax on employment has little to commend it.

The other alternative is to get back to the principles of insurance embodied in the Act of 1911, of securing to every workman, in virtue of contributions made by him while working and by his employer, the right to a definite income for a limited period of unemployment. This involves, on the one hand, an attempt to adjust contributions to risks of unemployment and, on the other hand, the organization of some kind of relief to be given to those who run out of insurance.

The first of these consequential requirements presents no serious difficulties. Even though it be decided, as possibly it must be decided, that differentiation of the stamps to be affixed to unemployment books is not practicable, except for very broad distinctions – such as that between agriculture and industry – other modes of differentiation remain. The regular workmen's case can be met by refunds, like that given at the age of sixty in the Act of 1911. Industries and employers with unemployment above the average can be made to pay for it, as is suggested later, by any one of several devices. The possibilities of raising money to pay for unemployment are not exhausted by the plan borrowed from Germany in 1911, of requiring an adhesive stamp to be stuck on a contribution card for each week of employment.

The second consequential requirement is more troublesome; it means carrying out some reform of the Poor Law in relation to the able-bodied. This was postulated alike in the first part of this volume and in both Reports of the Poor Law Commission. Here lies the main difference of principle between the alternatives named above. The giving of money without other conditions during unemployment was justified in 1911 as a means of tiding over temporary depression men who needed nothing but tiding over; the assumption that under-lay limitation of the period of benefit was that those who remained unemployed beyond a certain time needed something more than tiding over in their own trades and places. Prolonged unemployment suggested that those suffering from it were superfluous, or out of place, or unfit; it would tend to make them unfit if they were not so already. For such men, as Mr Davison puts it, 'maintenance is not enough'. The main argument for the second alternative is that it would make easier the distinction between industrial maintenance, by spreading of wages, and relief which sooner or later must involve pressure on the individual to change his trade or place or ways. It would, no doubt, be possible in a pure relief system to graduate the terms of relief, and give it on terms of increasing discipline for prolonged unemployment. But though possible it would be much harder. What does not seem possible, without grave damage, is to continue any longer to mix up relief with insurance. The payment of insurance contributions does not now materially add to the self-respect of the workman and does not give him and his employer any sense of being interested in the solvency of the scheme. But the ghost of insurance rights haunts the scheme and makes it hard to discrimi-nate between those for whom maintenance is enough and those who need something more.

C3   Mass Unemployment Caused by 'an Abnormal rise of Real Wages' (pp. 359–60, 367–71)

Changes of industrial structure have become sudden instead of slow and account for some of the difference between prewar and postwar unemployment. It is hard to believe that they explain it all. In the first place, the war is now more than ten years behind us. If nothing were needed but a readjustment of the quality of the labour supply to new conditions, it would be natural to expect more progress than appears towards absorption of the unemployed. In the second place, unem-ployment appears too widespread to be explained by depression of particular trades. If nothing but changes of structure in a healthy industrial system were at work, there should be somewhere, as the complement to the declining industries and districts, other industries and districts with a swiftly expanding demand for labour. This, however, is just what in Britain today it seems impossible to find. There are some districts with less unemployment than others, but are there any with unemployment as low as or lower than what was normal before the war? There are some new industries growing as the old ones decline, but the growth of employment in them is not such as to encourage easy optimism . . .

Today the real cost of labour to the employer for each unit of output may be as much as one-sixth or more higher than before the war . . . The widespread enduring unemployment that we find in Great Britain is just what we should expect to find as the result of an abnormal rise of wages, unaccompanied by an equal rise of productivity or cheapening of capital . . . Apart from passing trade depressions, it is fair to say that rises of real wages before the war followed on increases of productivity, were made possible by such increases, and kept within limits set by them. The war and its aftermath present a different picture.

To begin with, in the war itself, consumption was divorced from production. The nation lived beyond its national income, lived well on savings and on borrowings. When the war ended, it had standards of life bearing no necessary relation to what it could produce, and had at the same time a sense of needing a rest from wartime exertions. To this wartime dislocation of standards succeeded the boom and depression of 1920–1, with a catastrophic fall of prices. The fall of money wages was much less and was checked sooner. The return to the gold standard for 1925 gave a fresh downward kick to prices while money wages remained unchanged, that is to say, real wages rose further. For in the mean time two new factors had come in to make money wages less plastic downwards. One was the growth of trade unionism and collective bargaining; the other was the generalization of unemployment insurance in 1920 and its conversion into unlimited relief, by extended benefit in 1921 and by statute in 1927. Of the former Professor Clay writes that 'there are few important gaps left in the provision for the settlement of wages by collective bargaining in Great Britain'. Of the latter Mr Rowe writes that 'unemployment insurance has almost completely abolished the fear of blackleg labour by the unemployed, however numerous' and 'has enormously strengthened the bargaining power of trade unionism'.

'This postwar disregard of unemployment in wage negotiations', infers Professor Clay, 'is the principal and direct explanation of the loss of plasticity in wage rates.'

The movements of wages and prices since the war and the corresponding movements of unemployment are shown graphically in the chart below. The beginning of the chart, up to 1925, is in substance the same as that given by M. Rueff, with a revision of wage figures suggested by Professor Bowley; the end of the chart deals with years not covered by M. Rueff. The curve of wages divided by prices and the curve of unemployment move uncannily together, from minima in the first part of 1920 to one maximum in 1921 and a secondary peak in 1922, thence downwards to 1924 and since then slowly upwards once more. The unemployment curve tends every now and again to lag just behind the other, at the minima of 1920 and 1924 and the maximum of 1922, as might be expected if it is an effect and the other the cause. The most considerable discrepancy of movement, in 1926, is what might be expected from the coal dispute of that year.

To sum up, postwar Britain presents two novel features – unexampled unemployment and a rise of real wages almost equally without

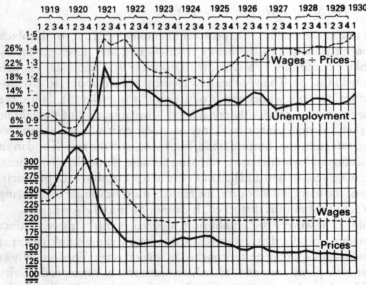

Fig 4.1 Wages, prices and unemployment in Britain from 1919 to 1929.

precedent. The former is most marked in the trades dependent on export. The latter has come about as a legacy of wartime dislocation rather than as an adjustment to improved economic conditions; it almost certainly outruns the increase in the productivity of labour. A rise of real wages of this character, and so occasioned, must naturally cause extensive and enduring unemployment, above all in export trades, either by raising the prices of British products in competition with those of other countries, or by reducing the margin from which capital is saved, or by causing a transference of capital to more remunerative use in other countries, or by a combination of two or more of these methods.

It is not easy, it might not be possible, to go farther than this in showing a causal connection between the rise of real wages and the rise of unemployment. It hardly seems reasonable, however, to doubt the connection. As a matter of theory, the continuance in any country of a substantial volume of unemployment which cannot be explained by specific maladjustments of place, quality and time, is in itself proof that the price being asked for labour as wages is too high for the conditions of the market; demand for and supply of labour are not finding their appropriate price for meeting.

C4   No Solution? (pp. 416–19)

For one new element . . . in postwar unemployment . . . for the black spots of mining and the heavy trades – national development by public expenditure is a remedy appropriate and necessary though limited in scope. To the other new element named above, to disequilibrium between wages and productivity, it is irrelevant, as are the other remedies previously considered – organization of the labour market, unemployment insurance or credit control – as are protection, safeguarding, Empire trade, free trade, and the rest. If and in so far as unemployment is now resulting because, through fall of prices, real wages have risen and become rigid at a point above the productivity of the marginal labourer, the remedy must be sought in restoring the equilibrium thus disturbed. It cannot be found elsewhere.

Since, however, the equilibrium desired involves three distinct elements – productivity, wages, and numbers seeking employment at those wages – it may be approached in several ways. Theoretically at least four plans are open: to reduce numbers, to raise productivity per head, to lower wages directly, to lower wages indirectly by raising prices. Practically the order of merit of these four plans is the inverse to their order of ease of accomplishment. Reduction of numbers by emigrating the unemployed surplus, if it could be done without other change in economic conditions, would be a full and immediate solution; unfortunately the married middle-aged industrial workers who are apt to form the surplus here seldom find it easy to gain admittance to other lands. At the other end of the list of plans comes indirect lowering of wages by rise of prices; this and the absorption of the unemployed in a temporary boom could probably be achieved very rapidly by a Government prepared for inflation, but the inevitable after-effects of such a policy rule it out. Substantially the choice lies between the second and third of the plans named – raising productivity to overtake wages or lowering wages to meet productivity. Here, too, the better plan is the harder. To concentrate, as a remedy for unemployment, on lowering wages, is open to several objections. One objection is that the swollen costs of production today include other elements than wages, e.g. interest on debentures which also have profited by fall of prices. Another and more important objection is that to admit reduction of wages as the prime means of reducing costs of production weakens the incentive to progress; the effect of such a doctrine on efficiency has been poignantly illustrated by the coal-mining industry. This objection is only one aspect of the fundamental objection of principle to lowering standards of life in face of a risk of overpopulation. On the other hand, increase of productivity cannot be achieved by wishing for it and cannot be achieved rapidly by continuing on old lines in industry. Output per head does now rise year by year as the result of technical and other improvements, but the rise since 1924 is put by the best authorities at certainly under 2 per cent a year. Even this has been offset of late by an equal or greater fall of prices raising real wages. To make an early impression on unemployment without lowering wages, progress on a different scale is needed. Whether and how it can be brought about must be left for discussion elsewhere and by others. Here three general observations must suffice.

First, since with the present levels of industrial efficiency and wages severe unemployment cannot be avoided, the obligation on those who wish to maintain wages is clear. The higher standard of life of those who are in regular work is to some extent won at the cost of unemployment of those who are not. The former and their leaders are in honour bound, not merely to remove restrictions on output, not simply to avoid opposing improvements of industrial technique and organization, but to further such improvements in every way within their power.

Second, even the most rapid rise of productivity may have little or no effect on the volume of unemployment, if its gains are at once swept away by wage demands. Output has somehow to be allowed to overtake consumption, and this means, at the very least, that for some time to come there should be no further general rises of wages.

Third, improvements of industrial efficiency, however beneficial in the end and however necessary today to diminish unemployment, often in the first instance make unemployment by displacing men from their previous occupations. In the long run, no doubt, such improvements increase rather than diminish the total demand for labour, but the new demands may be in other industries or places or for workpeople of a different kind from those who have lost employment. How soon, therefore, the labour displaced by rationalization or any other form of industrial progress can be reabsorbed is essentially a question of mobility. The old argument for labour market organization returns as always.

The main result of the fresh examination here made of unemployment should not be discouraging. In the concluding chapter of Part 1, the policies then proposed were summed up as making the supply of labour more capable of following and waiting for the demand – of following the demand through labour market organization, of waiting for it through insurance. To these policies another must now be added – that of adjusting production to standards of living or standards of living to production. But, with this addition, unemployment remains, in 1930 as in 1909, a problem of industry, not an Act of God.

Some things in Britain's destiny are beyond management by its governments and its leaders; the slow vast forces shaping and reshaping the economic structure of the world and the swift changes of personal desire that determine future numbers work uncontrollably, outside their reach or beneath their feet. But unemployment is not of these. It is no mysterious visitation, but in the main the consequence of our own choices, the measure of how our industry adjusts to the changing world. For one great industry the changes have been too catastrophic for adjustment and have left a disaster for which there is no full remedy. The problem of the ruined mining area stands by itself – an ill to make the best of till time ends it, by moving one by one all who can move, by expenditure in organizing such work as is possible for those who cannot move. Apart from this acute but limited problem, we know what to do if we wish to get back to the level of unemployment that ruled before the war; we must either lower our standards of life or bring production up to justify them. We know also what to do if we wish to bring unemployment below that level; carry out the main preventive policy of 1909 and organize completely the labour market, abolishing the hawking of labour and casual underemployment and the anarchic recruiting of trades and the blind choice of careers. These things cannot be done by wishing for them but, by fixed purpose, by willing means as well as ends, by counting and deciding to pay the price, they can be done. If we prefer not to do them, if we think the cost of curing unemployment too high, we may continue instead to pay for unemployment; the post-war situation puts frankly the question, how much unemployment we are prepared to carry in order to avoid surrender of standards of life once gained.

4D   Keynes's Break and Beveridge's Instruments

Source: Full Employment in a Free Society (1944)

D1   Keynes and 'the Revolution of Economic Thought' (pp. 105–6, 107, 108–9)

Unemployment before the First World War appeared as an evil calling for remedy, but not as the most serious economic problem of its time. That it was this between two wars will be denied by few. The average rate of unemployment in Britain, that is to say the percentage of persons seeking work who could not find it, was between two and three times, most probably two and a half times, as high between the wars as it had been before the First World War. But doubling or trebling the rate of unemployment means much more than doubling or trebling the misery of unemployment. With unemployment at 5 per cent or less, the bulk of it consists of short interval unemployment of people who have not been idle long and can hope shortly to return to work. Unemployment at 15 per cent includes many who have been unemployed for long periods and have lost or are losing hope, as well as bodily vigour and the habit of work. Unemployment in Britain after the First World War had a new and grimmer face.

In this respect the experience of Britain accords with that of other industrial countries having similar economic systems . . . Nor is there room for reasonable doubt as to the direction in which the remedy must be sought. The two approaches to the problem of unemployment in my first study of 1909 and in J. M. Keynes's *General Theory* of 1936, are not contradictory but complementary. The level of employment and unemployment at any time depends on the one hand, on the demand for the products of industry, and on the other hand, on the manner in which industry responds to the demand. In 1909, I assumed, in accord with all academic economists and most practical men, that, apart from the trade cycle, demand would look after itself. I was concerned mainly with the way in which industry responded to demand; the results of that study were summed up in its title – *Unemployment: a problem of industry*. The revolution of economic thought effected by J. M. Keynes, aided by the experience of the thirties, lies in the fact that adequate demand for labour is no longer taken for granted. The Keynesian analysis leads to the conclusion that, even apart from cyclical depression, there may be chronic or nearly chronic deficiency in the total demand for labour, with full employment a rare fleeting accident. J. M. Keynes is not concerned with frictional unemployment at all: it is excluded formally from his study. The Keynesian analysis does not deny the importance of disorganization of the labour market as a cause of unemployment. My first study did not deny the possibility of deficiency in total demand for labour.

The new facts and the new theories of unemployment lead to the same conclusion: that an unplanned market economy is less automatically self-adjusting at a high level of employment than had been supposed in earlier times. Before the First World War, there was no full record of unemployment in any country in the world. But the reality, persistence, and generality of the international trade cycle are established. For this period it is arguable, though there are few, if any, facts to support the argument, that adequate demand for the products of industry was attained at the top of each cyclical boom, but, at the highest, this meant for Britain only for one year in six between 1883 and 1914. And even in this period there was structural unemployment due to the uncontrolled shifting of industry from one part of the country to another; though the general level of unemployment was much lower in 1913 than in 1937, the differences between one region and another were equally marked in the two years.

For the period between the two World Wars, there is a full record of severe unemployment in Britain and there are records which leave little doubt that during the nineteen-thirties unemployment was substantially more serious in the United States than in Britain, to compensate for its lesser seriousness before 1930. In this period each country experienced a particularly severe return of cyclical fluctuation; though more violent in Britain than anything experienced, at least since 1850, this fluctuation was of the same general character as former fluctuations – was a fresh manifestation of the international trade cycle. The boom which ended this fluctuation in 1937 and heralded the beginning of a new depression, left 10 per cent of the labour force unemployed in Britain and about 12 per cent unemployed in the United States. As regards the United States, this high unemployment at the top of a cyclical boom cannot be explained as due to structural unemployment. If that explanation is offered for Britain, the answer is that failure for nearly twenty years to deal with structural unemployment is in itself a serious weakness of the unplanned market economy. Because such demand as was generated by this economy for the products of industry was so weak, it was not effective in overcoming industrial friction; because it was so badly located with reference to the supplies of available labour, it made that friction abnormally strong.

The need for a new attack on the problem of unemployment cannot be denied today, except in a mood of unthinking optimism. The attack must be on three lines. There is unemployment due to chronic or recurrent deficiency of demand. There is unemployment due to misdirection of demand. There is unemployment due to the degree to which the labour market remains unorganized and to the manner in which particular industries respond to demand. The reduction of unemployment to a harmless minimum requires, therefore, measures of three kinds; measures to ensure sufficient steady demand for the products of industry; measures to direct demand with regard to the labour available; measures to organize the labour market and to assist the supply of labour to move in accord with demand.

4E Policies for Full Employment

Source: Full Employment in a Free Society (1944)

E1 The Meaning of Full Employment and a Measure of It (pp. 18–19, 121, 129)

What is meant by 'full employment', and what is not meant by it? Full employment does not mean literally no unemployment; that is to say, it does not mean that every man and woman in the country who is fit and free for work is employed productively on every day of his or her working life. In every country with a variable climate there will be seasons when particular forms of work are impossible or difficult. In every progressive society there will be changes in the demand for labour, qualitatively if not quantitatively; that is to say, there will be periods during which particular individuals can no longer be advantageously employed in their former occupations and may be unemployed till they find and fit themselves for fresh occupations. Some frictional unemployment there will be in a progressive society however high the demand for labour. Full employment means that unemployment is reduced to short intervals of standing by, with the certainty that very soon one will be wanted in one's old job again or will be wanted in a new job that is within one's power . . .

Full employment in this Report means more than that in two ways. It means having always more vacant jobs than unemployed men, not slightly fewer jobs. It means that the jobs are at fair wages, of such a kind, and so located, that the unemployed men can reasonably be expected to take them; it means, by consequence, that the normal lag between losing one job and finding another will be very short.

The proposition that there should always be more vacant jobs than unemployed men means that the labour market should always be a seller's market rather than a buyer's market . . . For this, on the view of society underlying this Report – that society exists for the individual – there is a decisive reason of principle. The reason is that difficulty in selling labour has consequences of a different order of harmfulness from those associated with difficulty in buying labour. A person who has difficulty in buying the labour that he wants suffers inconvenience or reduction of profits. A person who cannot

136

sell his labour is in effect told that he is of no use. The first difficulty causes annoyance or loss. The other is a personal catastrophe. This difference remains even if an adequate income is provided, by insurance or otherwise, during unemployment; idleness even on an income corrupts; the feeling of not being wanted demoralizes. The difference remains even if most people are unemployed only for relatively short periods. As long as there is any long-term unemployment not obviously due to personal deficiency, anybody who loses his job fears that he may be one of the unlucky ones who will not get another job quickly. The short-term unemployed do not know that they are short-term unemployed till their unemployment is over.

The human difference between failing to buy and failing to sell labour is the decisive reason for aiming to make the labour market a seller's rather than a buyer's market. There are other reasons, only slightly less important. One reason is that only if there is work for all is it fair to expect workpeople, individually and collectively in trade unions, to co-operate in making the most of all productive resources, including labour, and to forgo restrictional practices. Another reason, related to this, is that the character and duration of individual unemployment caused by structural and technical change in industry will depend on the strength of the demand for labour in the new forms required after the change. The greater the pace of the economic machine, the more rapidly will structural unemployment disappear, the less resistance of every kind will there be to progress. Yet another reason is the stimulus to technical advance that is given by shortage of labour.

In so far as room is left for change and for freedom of movement from job to job, room is left for some unemployment. The aim of this Report is expressed in numerical terms in paragraph 169 as a reduction of unemployment to not more than 3 per cent, as compared with the 10 to 22 per cent experienced in Britain between the wars. But though the Report assumes the continuance of some unemployment and suggests a figure of 3 per cent, it is the essence of the proposals made in the Report that this 3 per cent should be unemployed only because there is industrial friction, and not because there are no vacant jobs. For men to have value and a sense of value there must always be useful things waiting to be done, with money to pay for doing them. Jobs, rather than men, should wait.

Three per cent of unemployment means 97 per cent of employment. If that were achieved, by how much would the material output of the community be increased? Ninety-seven per cent in employment, as compared with the 86 per cent which was the average between the wars, means raising the numbers in employment by about one-eighth . . . Exact estimates of how much production could be increased by a policy of full employment are impossible, but it is probably fair to set the factors making for a more than proportionate increase against those making for a less than proportionate increase and to assume for the purpose of general argument, that an increase of one-eighth in employment resulting from vigorous demand for labour would lead to a roughly proportionate increase in production. In terms of output just before this war, this would have meant adding something like £500 million a year at prewar prices to the value of the national product.

E2 *Budgetary Policy and Full Employment (pp. 147–50, 186–7)*

After the Government has accepted the principle of budgeting for full employment, that is to say, of budgeting to the datum of manpower, it still has to decide many further questions; as between mainly planned and unplanned outlay for maintenance of employment; as to the extent to which it shall rely upon making public outlay itself, and upon influencing private outlay; as to the division of outlay between consumption and investment; and finally as to the extent to which the means of outlay, whether private or public, shall be provided by taxation and by borrowing respectively. On what grounds are these and other practical decisions to be made? In other words, what new rules of national finance should replace the old rule of public finance, named and discarded above, of reducing State expenditure to a minimum and of balancing the Budget each year? The answer lies in laying down three rules of national finance, in order of importance. The first rule is that total outlay at all times must be sufficient for full employment. This is a categorical imperative taking precedence over all other rules, and overriding them if they are in conflict with it. The second rule is that, subject to this overriding categorical imperative, outlay should be directed by regard to social priorities. The third rule is that subject both to the first and second rule, it is better to provide the means for outlay by taxing than by borrowing.

The first rule is abolute. It is better to employ people on digging holes and filling them up again, than not to employ them at all; those who are taken into useless employment will, by what they earn and spend, give useful employment to others. It is better to employ people, however the money for paying their wages is obtained, than not to employ them at all; enforced idleness is a waste of real resources and a waste of lives, which can never be made good, and which cannot be defended on any financial ground. The second rule is hardly less important. The object of all human activity is not employment but welfare, to raise the material standard of living and make opportunities for wider spiritual life. For these purposes the wise direction of outlay and so of employment, in the general interest of the community, is only less important than adequacy of outlay as a whole. The third rule is of an altogether minor order of importance. The State in matters of finance is in a different position from any private citizen or association of private citizens; it is able to control money in place of being controlled by it. Many of the mistakes of the past have arisen through failure to make this fundamental distinction. Spending in excess of current income and borrowing have altogether different implications for the State than for private citizens . . . An internal national debt increases the incomes of some citizens by just as much as the taxation necessary to pay interest and sinking fund on the debt decreases the incomes of other citizens; it does not and cannot reduce the total wealth of the community. Nor, having regard to the actual scale of expenditure that will be needed to maintain full employment, is there any reasonable ground for fearing that national debt incurred for this purpose in peace will ever rise to a point making it necessary to raise fresh taxes . . . taking into account prospective changes in population, in productivity, and in working hours, as well as foreseeable changes of Government expenditure on pensions, education etc., and assuming an average rate of interest of 2 per cent, the National Debt could be expanded at the rate of not less than £775 million a year from 1948 (taken as the beginning of the reconstruction period) to 1970, without involving on that account any increase of tax rates to meet the additional charge for interest. This is a rate of borrowing far in excess of anything that would be needed to sustain full employment in peacetime. A policy of continuous borrowing, on a more reasonable scale adequate for all possible requirements, is consistent with a steady reduction of the burden of the debt on the taxpayer. To submit to unemployment or slums or want, to let children go hungry and the sick untended, for fear of increasing the internal national debt, is to lose all sense of relative values.

Nevertheless, there are good reasons for meeting State outlay, as far as is practicable, from current revenue raised by taxation, rather than by borrowing. The main reason is the objection to increasing the numbers and wealth of rentiers, that is to say of people with legal claims against the community entitling them to live at the cost of the community of the day without working, although they are of an age and capacity to work. This reason is irrespective of the purposes for which the money is borrowed; it is a ground both for keeping taxation as high as it can be kept without stifling desirable enterprise and for making the rate of interest continually lower, till in the phrase of J. M. Keynes the 'euthanasia of the rentier' is accomplished. A policy of cheap money should be regarded as an integral part of any plan for full employment. A subsidiary reason is that borrowing to meet State expenditure, in place of meeting it from current revenue, enables the Government of the day to avoid the unpopular task of taxing and the loss of votes from this unpopularity. In other words it increases the opportunities of general political bribery. For these two reasons, orthodox finance, so long as it does not conflict with either the first or the second of the new rules of national finance, has much to commend it.

But rigidly orthodox finance, in the sense of an annually balanced budget, involves, in the political and economic conditions of Britain, an impracticable route to full employment. Nor is there any need to struggle with the difficulties of such a route. A large proportion of the public outlay most needed in the near future will result in the production of durable goods – houses and their labour-saving equipment, hospitals and clinics, schools for scholars of all ages, means of transport. Few people will expect that all these should be paid for out of current revenue; they represent capital rather than current expenditure and are the natural subject of borrowing. The real problem is to decide what should be the proper relation between the tax revenue and the current expenditure of the State. And the first step in making that decision rightly is to approach the problem, not from the angle of public finance, but from the angle of social policy. Taxation in future should be looked on as a means of reducing private expenditure on consumption and thereby freeing real resources for other uses. There may be situations when the State should raise considerably more money in taxation than is needed to cover its current expenditure, not, however, for the traditional reason of reducing the national debt, but for the economic reason of securing real resources for purposes of high social priority. There may be other situations when there are no investment or other projects of high social priority, and when taxes should be reduced, so as to allow more of the national resources to be devoted to purposes of current private consumption. Decision as to the extent to which tax revenue should exceed or fall short of the current expenditure of the State depends upon the circumstances of the time. At all times, however, it should be based, not on considerations of finance and budgetary equilibrium, but on weighing of priorities, that is to say on social and economic policy.

This means that the decision as to how money required for public outlay should be raised depends really on the decision as to how money can be spent to best advantage, by public authorities and by private citizens together. On this there arise two related issues; we have to decide between outlay which is mainly or wholly planned and outlay which is wholly or mainly unplanned, being left to the decisions of individual citizens; we have to decide (or divide) between consumption outlay, producing goods and services for immediate enjoyment, and investment outlay, producing physical equipment which will yield goods and services for enjoyment over a period of time. On each of these issues the decision has to be reached, not on general principles, but on facts of time and place, that is to say, on the circumstances of the country in which the issue arises at the time when it arises.

As regards the first issue, between planned and unplanned outlay, so long as there are definite common objectives which, when stated, commend themselves to the good sense of the community, planned outlay is to be preferred to unplanned outlay. So long as there are things as to which most people agree that they ought to be done, it is better to decide and to plan to do them than to take the chance that they may get done without planning. That is what happens in war; everyone is agreed as to the need of waging war successfully and the whole effort of the community gets planned to that end. The view underlying this Report is that for the country and period for which this Report is designed – Britain immediately after the transition from war to peace – there are common objectives calling for planning, as decisively as war calls for planning today. This period is envisaged here as a reconstruction period – twenty years or more or less – following the transition period – perhaps two or three years – that it may take to pass from war to peace after total war ends. In that reconstruction period, there are certain things which must be done. We have to bring about an even balance of our payments abroad, because we cannot live indefinitely on the savings of former generations. We have to destroy the giant evils of Want, Disease, Squalor and Ignorance, which are a scandal and a danger. We have to raise our output per head by improving our mechanical equipment, because that is the only way to the steadily rising standard of life, material and spiritual, which we desire. These are common objectives which, when stated, command general assent; all of them involve planned rather than unplanned outlay.

. . . it is arguable that freedom of citizens to spend their money well or ill is an essential citizen liberty and that, in so far as bad spending results from high pressure salesmanship, the remedy is not to restrict the liberty of citizens but to control the methods of salesmanship, by such measures as regulation of hire purchase or conversion of industrial assurance into a public service. [But] there are vital things needing to be done to raise the standard of health and happiness in Britain which can only be done by common action, which in a community where democracy is so well established as in Britain will be secured in accord with the wishes of the citizens by the democratically controlled State.

Some redistribution of private incomes, increasing the propensity to consume, should be part of a full employment policy. But it cannot be the whole of that policy or its main instrument. For technical and for moral reasons alike, the State, if it undertakes the responsibility of ensuring sufficient total outlay for full employment, must concern itself also with the direction of outlay. The right division between the scope of the State and of the private citizens in this matter may well be found in the application of the principle of a social minimum. In the total outlay directed to maintain full employment, priority is required for a minimum for all citizens of housing, health, education and nutrition, and a minimum of investment to raise the standard of life of future generations. The democratic state must be guided, and can safely be guided by social priorities up to that minimum. The scope for free action by the citizens is in spending above that minimum.

E3 The International Preconditions of Keynesianism (pp. 209–10, 218)

The dependence of the classical argument for the advantages of free international trade and the disadvantage of almost all forms of protection upon the assumption of full employment is a point . . . emphasized by J. M. Keynes . . . A country suffering from depression and unemployment may want a surplus of exports over imports as a way of getting out of depression, and in order to secure this export surplus, it may by tariffs and in other ways, restrict drastically its current imports. This is a policy of each country helping itself at the expense of others which, if practised by all countries, can lead to no positive result for any of them. But for every depressed industrial country, the temptation to such a course is strong, and may often be irresistible. In the great depression of the nineteen-thirties, it proved irresistible for nearly every country in the world.

Avoidance of mass unemployment is an assumption of uncontrolled international trading, in a much more important sense than it is an assumption of Social Security. In relation to the Plan for Social Security set out in my earlier Report, Assumption C – that mass unemployment is prevented – means merely that, if there is mass unemployment, Social Security by income maintenance does not meet the needs; unemployment benefit is adequate treatment only for short interval unemployment. In relation to international trade, avoidance of mass unemployment in each of the main industrial countries is an underlying assumption in a much fuller sense; the whole economic relationship of different countries to one another depends primarily on the success which each of them achieves in securing a high stable level of employment at home. Plans for international trade must be different, according as we do or do not expect the chief industrial countries of the world to be successful in avoiding mass unemployment.

A suitable economic policy obviously cannot mean that all nations must have the same domestic economic structure. Trade must be made possible between countries, some of which are socialist while others are capitalist; some of which are democratic while others are authoritarian; some of which favour free trade or low tariffs while others are highly protectionist. A suitable economic policy can only mean a policy which is free from sudden and unpredictable changes;

a policy which does not put undue strains and stresses upon the rest of the world; in short, an economic good neighbour policy. General multilateral trading, as practised under the Gold Standard and as envisaged in the expert proposals for establishment of what is for practical purposes an international currency, is possible only if three conditions, or assumptions, are fulfilled: first, each of the participating nations must aim at full employment within its borders and must do so without relying on export surpluses as the principal means to full employment. Second, each of the participating nations must be prepared to balance its accounts with the rest of the world; for that purpose any nation which, for any reason, systematically sells abroad in goods or services more than it buys from abroad, and so has an export surplus, must be prepared to grant long-term loans sufficient to enable the rest of the world to pay for those exports, without losing gold or other reserves essential for international liquidity. Third, each of the participating nations must aim at a certain stability of economic behaviour – continuity in tariff, subsidy, foreign exchange and other economic policies – and must refrain from introducing important changes in these policies without prior consultation with the other participants.

5

The Role of Voluntary Action

Although Beveridge believed in minimal state intervention he was not an uncritical enthusiast or apologist for the market. He deprecated the selfish motive and believed in 'making and keeping something other than pursuit of gain as the dominant force in society' (extract 5B). It has already been argued that Beveridge's third report, *Voluntary Action* (1948), is a crucial lost text which presents Beveridge's blueprint for the development of private welfare provision in a society where the state had accepted an enlarged responsibility for full employment and social security. With its accompanying volume of evidence this text directly provides an analysis of the survival prospects of the friendly societies which had traditionally organized private health insurance on a non-profit-making basis. Although the friendly societies have since declined towards extinction, *Voluntary Action* is a text of unique value because Beveridge here develops his vision of how a large 'voluntary action' sector could function as a kind of buffer zone between the state and the market.

As a prelude we need to examine the nature of Beveridge's critique of the market. Extract 5A reprints a neglected section of the 1942 social insurance report, Appendix D, where Beveridge criticized 'industrial assurance' or the business of selling life insurance to the working class. Here provision of a basic service has been left to the market and Beveridge argued the results were wasteful and irrational. In this business working-class households took out life policies with private insurance companies who paid a small lump sum at death; the policies covered the cost of a decent funeral in return for premiums of a few pence paid each week on the doorstep. This was big business; industrial life assurance was the dominant form of private saving in the working class and in the late 1930s working-class households paid out more each week in private insurance premiums than they did on state social insurance contributions (*SIAS*, 1942, p. 113). But, as earlier investigators had proved, industrial life assurance was also poor value for money. Administrative expenses were high because an army of collectors was employed to collect weekly premiums; administration took 7s 6d (37p) in each pound of premium paid (extract 5A). Furthermore, life cover was not maintained if the working-class household could not keep up the regular weekly payments and the policy lapsed. Lapses were encouraged (or at least condoned) by the many collectors who were rewarded for securing new business; in 1929, 444,000 Royal Liver company policies lapsed while the company's agents sold no fewer than 810,000 new policies (*SIAS*, 1942, p. 266). This 'overselling' represented a pathological adaptation to the difficulty of extracting life insurance premiums from a social group whose incomes left little or no room for regular saving.

In his 1942 report on social insurance, Beveridge followed through the logic of this critique and proposed that the industrial life assurance business should be socialized (extract 5A). The *raison d'être* of the private business would be removed if the state paid a death grant to all. The expense of a decent funeral was a basic necessity, and Beveridge argued that provision for this expense was therefore a natural and proper part of the universal minimum which social insurance should provide; 'everybody in this country will die some time and everybody will need, even if he does not enjoy, his funeral' (*Why I am a Liberal*, 1945, p. 72). The case for a state grant was strengthened because the state could provide the necessary cover in an efficient and cost effective way; if death benefits were tagged on to a compulsory social insurance scheme, Beveridge argued that administrative costs could be reduced to around 2 per cent of income, compared with 30–40 per cent in industrial life assurance (*Why I am a Liberal*, 1945, pp. 72–3). Beveridge's usual stance was then to leave any provision above the minimum to private enterprise and the market. But in this instance he proposed to go much further. After the introduction of state death benefit, the army of door-to-door collectors would no doubt be used to sell supplementary insurance cover on life and health. The development of this business should not be left in the hands of private insurance companies; it should be conducted by an Industrial Assurance Board which would be given a statutory monopoly on the use of collectors (extract 5A). The interesting point is that Beveridge did not propose to nationalize the private insurance companies. The business of selling ordinary life insurance to the middle classes who paid monthly or annual premiums (without benefit of collectors) would be completely unaffected by the changes Beveridge proposed.

Beveridge's design for private life assurance in the welfare state was never implemented; only growing affluence and more sophisticated payments arrangements have slowly diminished the relative importance of what is now called 'home insurance' and the expense ratio remains scandalously high whenever insurance companies sell to the poor. But the Beveridge design is interesting because it shows that he does not rest the case for socialization of industrial life assurance entirely on arguments about waste and inefficiency. The case for socialization is argued within the political problematic of liberal collectivism where Beveridge had to justify treating two distinct categories of insurance consumer in quite different ways; effectively a system of protective tutelage was to be organized for the working class while the middle class was to be allowed freedom of contract on a *caveat emptor* basis. Beveridge argued that the characteristics of the working-class consumer of insurance and the relation of the consumer to the product and to the agent who sold insurance was such as to justify a kind of intervention which would be inappropriate in the case of a middle-class consumer of ordinary life insurance.

> Life insurance is not like other commodities, because those who insure make their choice once and for all when they take out a policy . . . Industrial assurance, that is to say life assurance among people of limited means . . . is different from ordinary life assurance, because those who undertake the latter have both, as a rule, less limited means and the possibility of recourse to independent advice. The consumers of industrial assurance have not this recourse; they should be guided in their choice of insurance by advice that is wholly disinterested. (extract 5A)

There was a strong and persuasive case for tutelage of the uninformed working-class consumer of life insurance who entered into a long-term contract which could not be easily re-negotiated. But the case for middle-class saving was never argued and rested on an idealization. Beveridge represented insurance provision as 'the function of the individual, that is to say it is a matter of free choice and voluntary insurance' (*SIAS*, 1942, p. 121). But the dominant forms of middle-class saving did not represent free contracts which were entirely in the private sector. Much middle-class saving was not voluntary; even in the 1940s pension provision through compulsory superannuation schemes was quite common for such groups. Many forms of middle-class saving were also dependent on the state; for example, substantial tax concessions were offered to those who entered into life insurance contracts. Tax-subvented private occupational welfare existed before the Second World War and it expanded massively in the postwar period; half the working population is now enrolled in occupational pension schemes and company cars account for more than half the new vehicles sold in Britain. If an unregulated private welfare system expanded in Britain after 1945 that was partly because Beveridge, who never recognized its existence, never made any proposals for regulating private welfare.

If Beveridge did not anticipate that private provision would take the form of occupational welfare, that was because he put his faith in the capacity of 'voluntary action' to create a large buffer zone between the state and the market. Against this background it is instructive to compare the third report of 1948 on voluntary action with the two earlier reports on social insurance and full employment in 1942 and 1944. The first two reports are impressive partly because they are so incisive about objectives and techniques. But this incisiveness is completely absent from the third report where objectives are usually general and techniques are seldom specified. In one account of the possibilities (see extract 1E) Beveridge supposed that whereas the state provided money, voluntary action could provide services. But it was never clear how the existing institutions of voluntary action could be directed into new forms of activity like the construction of sheltered housing, the running of old people's homes or the provision of non-profit-making holiday camps. In another formulation (see extract 5B) Beveridge supposed that voluntary action could find a 'limitless field' in the provision of worthwhile leisure pursuits for a working class which had been exploited by the promoters of football pools and dog races. But Beveridge never explained how resources could be effectively mobilized for this moral crusade.

When Beveridge failed to specify pertinent techniques of voluntary action which could realize his worthy general objectives, these objectives were reduced to the level of rhetoric about 'a society which gives itself up to the domination of the business motive is a bad society. We do not put first things first in putting ourselves first' (extract 5B). There must be a strong suspicion that the whole field for voluntary action exists in a residual way that answers only the needs of Beveridge's broader ideology which both distrusts the market and seeks to limit the state's activities. This is clear when Beveridge was, for example, arguing that voluntary action should organize services such as citizens' advice bureaux; this was appropriate because Beveridge believed that such services should and could not be organized by the state or private business (extract 5B). If friendly society provision of sickness insurance loomed large in the third report, that was partly because this was the one area of voluntary action where Beveridge had a properly worked-out position. Here Beveridge identified an institution and a service which already existed and might perhaps serve as an instrument through which the motive of mutual aid might be converted into a significant output of purposive voluntary action.

Beveridge had an idiosyncratic Manichaean view of capitalism; capitalism was the scene of eternal conflict between the motives of altruism and selfishness. The actors on this scene were institutions which in some metaphysical way could embody and express these motives. Industrial assurance companies were low expressions of the business motive; here 'the business motive has become dominant, and gain without limit has been sought by doing the simplest possible service' (*Voluntary Action*, 1948, p. 8). Friendly societies were high expressions of mutual aid; 'the friendly society movement is a democratic movement of Mutual Aid sprung from the working classes' (extract 5C). Beveridge accepted that friendly societies faced considerable difficulties in the late 1940s. They faced increasing competition from the state in sickness insurance which was their sole or main activity when as 'approved societies' after 1911 they had been comfortably integrated into the operation of state social insurance. After 1945 that changed when, contrary to Beveridge's 1942 recommendations, the state excluded the friendly societies from any role in the state scheme. Nevertheless, Beveridge remained optimistic about the prospects of the friendly societies.

The degree to which the friendly societies triumph over their difficulties will depend on their life and the spirit of service in them, on their being ready to meet new needs by new methods, in the old spirit of social advance by brotherly co-operation. That most of them will do so can be taken for certain. The greatest danger of the present situation is not on the side of the friendly societies. They will survive; if they did not do so, their place would be taken by new forms of voluntary organization. (*Voluntary Action*, 1948, pp. 83–4)

If Beveridge in *Voluntary Action* believed in a happy ending, the companion volume *Evidence for Voluntary Action*, which Beveridge edited, showed that was wishful thinking. It was certain that the friendly societies did not have the vitality to win out against the business motive. Within the field of private saving, the dominant role was occupied by other kinds of institution which served the motive of personal thrift without any pretence of mutuality. Official statistics published by the registrar of friendly societies showed that building societies and trustee savings banks had mobilized the largest funds. Within the lower income groups, saving through industrial assurance was much more important than saving through friendly societies; in the 1937–40 period, for example, the average annual premium income of the industrial assurance business exceeded the accumulated funds of the affiliated order type of friendly society.

It was also doubtful whether all the friendly societies any longer represented the motive of mutual aid. The strength of the personal thrift motive was demonstrated by developments inside the friendly society movement which included several different types of society. Beveridge favoured the affiliated order type of friendly society which maintained 'good fellowship in spite of growth' (*Voluntary Action*, 1943, p. 137). But in the period after 1914, the growth in friendly society membership and in financial resources had been entirely concentrated in the so-called Holloway and Deposit types of friendly society which were geared to personal saving because in these types of friendly society 'the investment interest earned was used to increase the members' individual surplus or deficit' (*Voluntary Action*, 1948, p. 329). Beveridge had to admit that the newer types of friendly society appealed to 'the motive of individual saving for emergencies' (*Voluntary Action*, 1948, p. 81) and the most successful Holloway societies were models of 'enterprising business' (*Voluntary Action*, 1948, p. 51).

The friendly society movement did have 8 million members but that strength was more apparent than real. If the friendly societies were to express and realize the ideal of mutuality, they needed an active membership of individuals who were committed to something more than drawing benefit when sick. But a Mass Observation survey, which Beveridge commissioned, showed that 'the membership of Friendly Societies today . . . is very largely a passive one' (extract 5D1). The social ritual of 'club night' had been a traditional feature of the affiliated orders and the small local societies. But this kind of club night was in decline (extract 5C2) and the majority of friendly society members, according to Mass Observation, knew very few members of their society and had no wish to meet others (extract 5D1). Understandably there was low participation in the political machinery of self-government; attendance at meetings was minimal and participation in elections derisory. The Mass Observation survey of one society concluded that seven out of eight members never attended meetings and merely paid their subscription (extract 5D2). Future prospects were even more gloomy because the friendly societies had an ageing membership and younger people had more pronounced 'negative attitudes' towards the movement.

When Beveridge published *Voluntary Action* in 1948, it was inevitable that friendly societies would decline towards extinction. Over the next thirty years, the decline of the movement was largely unremarked and unlamented. By the 1980s, it was difficult to find any reference to friendly societies outside the financial pages of the quality press which occasionally explained how friendly societies could be used as a tax shelter for personal savings. The institutions of working-class mutual aid have an after-life as adjuncts to middle-class individualism.

5A   Beveridge's Critique of Working-Class Life Assurance

Source: SIAS (1942), p. 249 and pp. 271–6 (Appendix D)

Industrial assurance is that class of life assurance in which the premiums are payable at intervals of less than two months and are received by means of collectors who make house-to-house visits for that purpose. This class of life assurance can be carried on either by an assurance company within the meaning of the Assurance Companies Act, 1909, or by a friendly society registered under the Friendly Societies Act of 1896. A company which carries on this business is termed 'an industrial assurance company'; it must be registered under the Companies Acts or the Industrial and Provident Societies Acts or be incorporated by special Act. A friendly society which carries on this business is termed a 'collecting society'. There are at the present time 14 companies and 146 societies conducting industrial assurance . . .

All the three independent committees which in the course of about forty years investigated the business of industrial assurance, while recognizing the need for the service rendered by it in providing for burial expenses, made strong criticisms both on the conduct of the business and as to the cost of the service . . .

To deny the good that there is in the development of life assurance by persons of limited means would be absurd. The question remains whether the defects of the business, as they have been pointed out by one independent inquiry after another, have now been remedied as completely as is possible or are likely to be remedied in time if the business continues on its present lines. The answer to that question, in view of the facts submitted above, must be negative, in relation both to cost of administration and to the extent of abortive insurance . . .

First, the essential universal need for direct funeral expenses, which is the starting-point of industrial assurance, can be met at a very small fraction of the cost of industrial assurance by compulsory social insurance. This is the ground for the proposal made as Change 18 in Part II, to include a universal funeral grant in the social insurance scheme. It is hard to see how the administrative cost of this could amount to more than about 6*d* (2p.) in the £, 2.5 per cent as compared with more than 37 per cent.

Second, the other needs – for personal expenditure in connection with death, for life assurance and for saving generally, being less uniform and less universal, are subjects for voluntary action rather than for compulsion. Voluntary insurance is necessarily and reasonably more costly in administration than compulsory insurance. But at least three great voluntary organizations now at work in Britain show the possibility of encouraging voluntary insurance or saving on a large scale among persons of limited means at a cost ratio far below that of industrial assurance. As is shown in Appendix E, the centralized friendly societies, with a membership of nearly 4,000,000, obtain contributions and administer a far more complicated system of benefits than that of industrial assurance at not much more than a quarter of the administrative cost of industrial assurance, 10 per cent, or 2/- in the £ of contributions . . . Hundreds of thousands of families with less than enough to live on contribute substantial proportions of their incomes to industrial insurance. From 30 per cent to 40 per cent or more of what they contribute goes in administrative expenses and profits.

Both the extent of abortive assurance and the evidence of the social surveys show the amount of industrial assurance today as excessive. That excess follows from the fact that it is a business with a strong internal pressure to develop in the interests of the staff or the interests of shareholders. Some amount of abortive insurance is inevitable in the life assurance of persons of limited means exposed to economic insecurity. That fact is a reason for keeping the amount of life assurance within the capacity of the buyers of insurance and removing the pressure to over-insurance which comes from the natural desire of the sellers of insurance for business gain.

The criticisms made upon industrial assurance in the past have not been met, and cannot be met while the system remains, as at present, a competitive business. The best hope of meeting them lies in following out some of the ideas which were present to the minds of the Cohen Committee.[1] That Committee, while ruling out nationalization of industrial assurance 'as it now exists' as not a practical proposition, added, 'Some of us, however, consider that the possibility of widening the scope of the present State Insurance Schemes so as to cover the contingencies now met by industrial assurance should be fully explored'. The Committee added as a final sentence to the main body of their Report, 'We are convinced that if the changes which the due protection of the assuring public demands cannot be effected by less drastic measures the difficulties in the transference of the business to a single organization to which we have referred at length will ultimately have to be faced.' This review leads to the suggestion that the only satisfactory solution of the problem of industrial assurance, retaining the good while curing the defects of the present system, will lie in following out the final hint of the Cohen Committee and converting industrial assurance from being a competitive sellers' business to being a monopoly consumers' service.

This suggestion involves no general conviction in favour of public monopolies or against private competition. Today it is recognized among reasonable men that there is a place for each of these methods in its appropriate sphere, and the choice between the two methods should depend upon the character of the work to be done. The proposal that life assurance among persons of limited means should be a public service rather than a competitive private business is based upon the special character of industrial assurance, as a business in which competition leads to overselling and as a business in which the seller's interest presents special danger to the consumer. Life insurance is not like other commodities, because those who insure make their choice once for all when they take out a policy. They cannot buy less insurance or another form of insurance next day or change their assurance company without loss, as next day they can substitute bacon for beef or change their grocer without loss. Industrial assurance, that is to say life assurance among people of limited means, is so different from most other commodities that it cannot safely be treated as an article of commerce. Industrial assurance is different from ordinary life assurance, because those who undertake the latter have both, as a rule, less limited means and the possibility of recourse to independent advice. The consumers of industrial assurance have not this recourse; they should be guided in their choice of insurance by advice that is wholly disinterested.

From these general arguments, the case for following to its logical conclusion of public monopoly the tendency of thought apparent in the Report of the Cohen Committee is strong in itself. The case is reinforced on practical grounds by consideration of two proposals made on other grounds, for changing the present system of approved societies (Report, paras 48–76) and for providing a funeral grant for every death as part of compulsory insurance (Report, paras 157–60). Both these proposals are an essential part of the Plan for Social Security. In theory, on the introduction of these measures, the industrial life offices might be left in their present form to cover the large and growing field that remains for voluntary insurance by persons of limited means.

Such a solution of the problem of industrial assurance is possible. It would, it is suggested, be unsatisfactory for several reasons . . . it would leave the present defects of industrial assurance – of overselling and excessive cost – in a narrower sphere, indeed, but unremedied. The way to economy in the use of collectors lies in rationalization and monopoly, not in competition. But a monopoly cannot be allowed to work for profits without control. The way to replacing the costly system of collectors gradually by more economical forms of insurance and saving is blocked so long as so many livelihoods depend on collection . . . . Voluntary insurance enabling the individual to make provision above the minimum for his special needs is an integral part of social security. The work of the industrial life offices, though marred by serious defects, though representing today an excessive drain on the limited resources of wage-earners, has made a contribution of great value in using and stimulating the spirit of thrift throughout the people. It has brought into being an army of collectors who in thousands of cases have become the friends of their clients. They can be used and should be used to better purpose than is the case today, to encourage fruitful saving, to play their part in bringing security to all . . . The industrial life offices cannot be used just as they stand for dealing with such problems; they cannot be used while they are businesses working for shareholders, or are associations of agents investing capital in books. But the men in these offices, their energies, abilities and experience should be used, for what they can do is needed.

These considerations lead to the proposal for setting up an Industrial Assurance Board with a statutory monopoly of the use of collectors. The Board would take over all the existing policies of industrial assurance and honour them. It would employ or compensate the staff. It would compensate the shareholders. It would take over all or part of the ordinary life assurance business of the industrial life offices, as might be found most convenient in each case. It would be authorized for the future to undertake new life assurance, whether with or without collection of premiums, subject to a limit of the amount assured, designed to restrict its clientele to persons of limited means; something like the present limit of £300 imposed on collecting societies would probably fit the case. The Board would work steadily to substitute direct payment of premiums for collection, to encourage socially desirable forms of insurance and thrift, to provide ways of insurance free from serious risk of lapsing. It would work under the general supervision of the Minister of Social Security but with a large measure of practical independence. It would use to the utmost the skill and energy which have gone to build up the industrial life offices. It would be not a Government department but a public service run on business lines.

5B The Motives of Mutual Aid and Philanthropy Expressed in Voluntary Action

Source: SIAS (1942), pp. 6–7
Voluntary Action (1948), pp. 8–10, 286–7, 321–2

The third principle is that social security must be achieved by co-operation between the State and the individual. The State should offer security for service and contribution. The State in organizing security should not stifle incentive, opportunity, responsibility; in establishing a national minimum, it should leave room and encouragement for voluntary action by each individual to provide more than that minimum for himself and his family . . .

The term 'Voluntary Action', as used here, means private action, that is to say action not under the directions of any authority wielding the power of the State. A study of Voluntary Action, without further limitation, would be as wide as life itself, covering all the undirected activities of individual citizens in their homes as well as outside their homes. This study is confined to Voluntary Action for a public purpose – for social advance. Its theme is Voluntary Action outside each citizen's home for improving the conditions of life for him and for his fellows . . .

Within that definition this Report is concerned specifically with action inspired by one or other of two main motives – Mutual Aid and Philanthropy. The first motive has its origin in a sense of one's own need for security against misfortune, and realization that, since one's fellows have the same need, by undertaking to help one another all may help themselves. The second motive springs from what is described in my Report on Social Insurance as social conscience, the feeling which makes men who are materially comfortable, mentally uncomfortable: to have social conscience is to be unwilling to make a separate peace with the giant social evils of Want, Disease, Squalor, Ignorance, Idleness, escaping into personal prosperity oneself, while leaving one's fellows in their clutches.

The Mutual Aid motive has given rise in Britain to citizen associations of many types . . . One type – the friendly society – is dealt with more fully than the rest, [because it] . . . has received less recent attention than it deserves; the last comprehensive study of this friendly society movement was made by a Royal Commission more than seventy years ago; the last book about it was published in 1891.

Most of the other leading forms of Mutual Aid association – trade unions, co-operative societies, building societies and so forth – have been the subject of abundant and more recent study . . .

The philanthropic motive has given rise in Britain to an almost infinite variety of institutions, societies and agencies. No attempt can be made here to do more than describe . . . their main types, with a few leading instances. One form of agency – the charitable trust – receives special notice, because, like the friendly societies, it has been unduly neglected hitherto . . .

Besides the two main motives, of Mutual Aid and of Philanthropy, the present study illustrates the working of two other motives. One is the motive of personal thrift, of saving to have money at one's own command, saving for personal independence; from the combination of this more individual motive with that of Mutual Aid spring some of the more interesting forms of voluntary association of citizens . . . The other is the business motive; the pursuit of a livelihood or of gain for oneself in meeting the needs of one's fellow-citizens; from the interplay of this motive with that of Mutual Aid or Personal Thrift have sprung organizations which are in some cases of portentous scale.

The world at large is engaged in debating, sometimes by reason and voting, sometimes in other ways, the advantages and disadvantages of private enterprise in business. This third Report is concerned with private enterprise, not in business but in the service of mankind, not for gain but under the driving power of social conscience. The need for private enterprise in that form is beyond debate . . . it involves making and keeping something other than pursuit of gain as the dominant force in society. The business motive, in the field covered by this Report, is seen in continual or repeated conflict with the philanthropic motive, and has too often been successful. The industrial assurance offices exploited successfully for gain a universal desire to avoid a pauper burial. They have been succeeded by the businesses of football pools, dog tracks and cinemas, all exploiting in different ways for personal gain the increased leisure of the people. The business motive is a good servant but a bad master, and a society which gives itself up to the dominance of the business motive is a bad society. We do not put first things first in putting ourselves first.

There is no need to argue at length the case for Voluntary Action in meeting the . . . needs arising out of the growing leisure of wage-earners and the growing complexities of modern life.

The last stage in totalitarianism would be reached if the use of his leisure were being arranged for each citizen by the State. But to leave this field to the play of the business motive, to the extent to which it is so left today, produces results which are far from cheering. It is difficult to imagine any standard by which transfer of time from even the dullest form of earning by work to the filling-in of a football coupon in hope of unearned wealth can be regarded as progress. The State should reconsider its attitude towards organized gambling and towards the facilities which it provides today for this particular form of private enterprise. But the main attack on wasteful or harmful use of leisure cannot, in a free society, be made by direct action of the State. It must depend on the development of alternative interests and free pursuits; it depends on education, in the widest sense of the term, at all stages of life, but above all in adolescence and after. The first call on the increased leisure of the democracy should be the fitting them for the responsibilities of democracy in choosing leaders and deciding on public issues. This is an interest of the State but should not be undertaken by the State. Here is a limitless field for Voluntary Action, assisted so far as is necessary but not controlled by the power of the State.

That citizens should find their way through the growing complexities of modern society is equally an interest of the State, but equally an interest which the State must seek to secure, not directly, but indirectly, through Voluntary Action . . . Advice to citizens must be given independently by other citizens. A public authority may provide the material means for citizens' advice bureaux but should no more control them than it controls universities.

5C   The Role of Friendly Societies

Source: Voluntary Action (1948)

C1   *Friendly Societies Can Combine Business and Benevolence, and Extend Mutual Aid to Philanthropy (pp. 83, 296–300)*

The friendly societies have a difficult time ahead of them, more so than the trade unions for whom sick and unemployment pay has been only a sideline, more so than the industrial life offices with their armies of collectors and their development into forms of life and endowment insurance which the State is leaving untouched. The degree to which the friendly societies triumph over their difficulties will depend on the life and the spirit of service in them, on their being ready to meet new needs by new methods, in the old spirit of social advance by brotherly co-operation. That most of them will do so can be taken for certain.

In spite of all that the State has done by social insurance to guarantee a minimum income for all at all times, there remains a large scope for insurance above the minimum. The British system of social insurance, unlike that of most other countries, is equalitarian, providing the same minimum for subsistence in sickness, unemployment and old age, without regard to differences in the income earned before, and the differing standards of life and expenditure to which that income has given rise. In giving to each one in social security according to his needs, Britain is nearer to the communist formula than is Soviet Russia, where pensions are related to previous earnings and may bear a higher proportion to those earnings for good service. The British system assumes a large measure of insurance to meet needs above the minimum. The making of provision above the minimum is left as the field of voluntary insurance.

There are many possibilities for exploration in this field; new forms of combining insurance and thrift; new endowment schemes, to keep for the children later, if not required at once; the additional resources made available by family allowances; new plans for special medical treatment beyond anything that is likely to be provided by the National Health Service. The proposal for a marriage grant, made in my Report, has not been accepted. Yet it is clear that insurance for a substantial sum to be drawn on marriage would solve many difficult problems and avoid recourse to the snares of hire purchase. Again, it is likely that the societies will find a strong demand for higher benefits in sickness, above what the State gives, particularly for a short period of incapacity.

In considering new developments of insurance, friendly societies should draw three lessons from the present study. The first lesson is the strong popular appeal of the combination of insurance and saving, which is shown by the persistence of dividing societies,[2] by the growth of societies based on the deposit and Holloway principles,[3] and by the adoption of these principles on the part of some societies, such as the Hearts of Oak and the Loyal Order of Shepherds, which had worked hitherto on conventional lines. The second lesson is that business interests have never found sickness insurance among wage-earners profitable. Here lies the outstanding advantage of the small local society, or branch of an affiliated order.[4] The third lesson is that in voluntary insurance for everything except sickness the friendly societies must realize that they are competing with the industrial life offices for business. They must be prepared to use business methods, including propaganda and advertising. They can offer to the public in many ways a better service than the business concerns, free of liability to shareholders, free of the heavy expense of collectors. But they should not wait for these advantages to be discovered for themselves by the public.

Finally, still within the field of provision in money, it is possible and natural for a friendly society, as it is not natural for a business concern, to give help in emergencies beyond any contract – to have funds for benevolence as well as for strict insurance.

In making provision in money to meet inequalities of circumstances, over and above what is guaranteed by the State, there is a large and familiar field still open to friendly societies. But the main unsatisfied needs that remain . . . require provision, not of money, but of service. To meet those needs is a harder and therefore more important task. Some of the matters dealt with in those chapters, such as the care of cripples or the blind, or the development of education, fall perhaps unduly far from anything that friendly societies have done in the past. But there are four points which might well prove suitable for friendly society action.

There is, first, the provision of suitable housing for old persons who can live independent lives. Many friendly societies have funds seeking investment. Housing societies need capital. Investment by a friendly society in housing societies designed to secure homes particularly for the members of the friendly society itself, would stimulate interest both centrally and locally in friendly society work.

There is, second, the urgent need for homes with service for old people who, while not in need of hospital treatment, cannot live independently. A number of the friendly societies now have convalescent homes. The need for such homes, for sick persons of working age, will presumably be diminished as the National Health Service

Act comes into action. The need for old people's homes with service will grow, as the number of old people grows.

There is, third, the provision of clubs. Many, perhaps most, friendly societies began as clubs. The need for clubs to give companionship for old people is greater today than ever it was. Young people with their families may not need clubs so much today as once they did; old people need them more than ever.

There is, fourth, the problem of making provision for the greatly increased demand for holidays. This is a need of the adolescent, of the young married couple, of the older married couple with children growing up, of the old as well; it runs through life. The commercial camps have shown the wisdom of making provision for holidays which give to the housewife and mother, as well as to the wage-earner, a relief from work, and not merely a change in the place of her work. But the commercial camps have a standard of expenditure and display which makes them too expensive for the mass of the people. Some of the non-commercial holiday associations have recognized the same family need and have set out to meet it at less expense. But the scale of their operations is too small for the numbers. Why should not the friendly societies set out to meet this need? In providing for holidays, for clubs, for old people's needs, the friendly societies would show themselves as societies concerned with all stages of life.

In relation to both the other great movements with which it has been compared above – trade unionism and consumers' co-operation – the friendly society movement has one distinctive advantage today. It stands outside party politics. Beyond what is needed to give it opportunities equal to its aims it has been and remains little concerned in getting action by the State. It can take as its function creation of channels for the spirit of voluntary service. The suggestion made in this chapter that friendly societies, not content with insurance for money, should widen their scope to include provision of service, is made both for its own sake and also because of its wider implications. The friendly society movement is a democratic movement of Mutual Aid sprung from the working classes. But Mutual Aid, in the more equal society of the future, must broaden into Philanthropy, into the promotion of social advancement, not simply each for himself, but for the whole of society . . . The friendly societies centrally might become guardians and promoters of democratic voluntary action. Locally they might become leaders or active

161

partners in every movement for social welfare or citizen service. That is the way to being more than organs for mutual insurance on business lines.

The essential business of friendly societies is Voluntary Action. Driven back on that once more, it rests with them to recapture for new ends the spirit of brotherly mutual service which made them the great pioneers of the past.

C2 *Friendly Societies as Social Clubs (pp. 60–1)*

But the friendly societies have been much more than agencies for dealing with averages by way of mutual insurance. They have been social clubs; they have been societies concerned with the general welfare of their members; they have been channels for the spirit of voluntary service.

The social side of the friendly society is typified by the regular 'club night' forming a feature of all the affiliated orders with their branches, and of the small local societies. The club night may be monthly, fortnightly or weekly; in the early days a meeting at each full moon was common, as enabling the brethren with less difficulty to find their way there – and back after a social evening. If the meeting is that of the branch of an affiliated order, it is normally introduced by a ritual, designed to impress upon members the high aims of the society and the respect which should be accorded to these aims. There may be passwords and signs as a condition of admittance. The room will be brightened by insignia and adorned by photographs of past officers of the branch, and by other memorials testifying to the honourable antiquity and usefulness of the society. The business of every meeting, in addition to correspondence and general questions, will include the administration of individual sick benefits, the branch receiving on that occasion the reports of the 'sick visitors', that is to say the individual members who have undertaken to call on sick brethren. In one of the principal orders, every meeting of every branch begins by the chairman putting three questions: first, whether any member has anything to propose that concerns the welfare of the order; second, whether he has anything to propose for the welfare of members individually; third, whether he has anything to propose that concerns the welfare of the branch. He repeats the same question at the end, and in this way gives an opportunity for every member to make recommendations concerning organization and business, as well as proposals of a benevolent character for the help of brothers who may have fallen into misfortune.

Undoubtedly the club night bulks less in the activity of friendly societies today than it did in the past. It is unknown to the large unitary society, whether that works on accumulating or deposit or Holloway principles. It draws a declining attendance in the orders. A branch of 150 members may produce a dozen or fewer attenders apart from the officers, and most of them will be middle-aged. But the club night continues as an integral part of the work of the orders, and of the local societies, as distinct from the large centralized organizations.

The welfare side of the friendly society is illustrated both by the friendly individual help which may spring up naturally at a meeting, and by action on a larger scale. A friendly society does not confine itself to making a business contract with its members. It is concerned with their welfare generally.

5D The Evidence of the Decay of Friendly Societies

Source: Evidence for Voluntary Action (1948)

D1 'Why People Join' (pp. 19–21)

A survey was also made of the opinions of some one hundred and fifty people who stated that they were members of friendly societies. A significant point emerged here. Out of the twenty-one insurance bodies to which these people belonged – all of which were stated by them to be 'friendly societies' – no less than nine were afterwards identified as being, not friendly societies proper, but collecting societies or insurance companies. The fact throws an interesting light upon the general ignorance of what a friendly society is; it is a notable reinforcement of Mass Observation's other findings. Fortunately the actual number of informants who made this mistake was not large, and conclusions are therefore not much vitiated.

These members were asked how they felt about their society, whether, on the whole, they approved or disapproved of the way in which it was functioning at present, why they had joined the society, how long they had been members, whether they knew or wished to know any of the other members of their group. They were asked, also, how they felt about attending meetings and taking part in the election of officials of their society; and, finally, whether they had any suggestions to make about ways in which the friendly society could contrive to serve a useful purpose in view of the wider provision for insurance now to be made by the State.

(a) WHY PEOPLE JOIN FRIENDLY SOCIETIES

The reasons most commonly given for membership of friendly societies are:

Economic security	Death and sickness benefits
	Benefits for dependants
	General provision for the future
Family influence	Members of family have 'always belonged'
	Parents obtained membership for children
Friends and work influence ..	Membership taken up on advice of friends or workmates
Friendly societies administer State Health Insurance ..	Membership a convenient way of obtaining National Health Benefit
Social amenities	Society had a 'club' appeal

Economic security reasons were advanced about twice as often as the 'family influnce' argument, and both these reasons were far more often given than any others. Only a very few people appear to have joined a friendly society with the idea of participating in the social functions which it might provide. A small number of people said they had joined because they believed that it was compulsory to do so, but this was almost invariably a 'younger member' attitude, as, to a large extent, was the assumption that the main object of the friendly society was to administer National Health Insurance . . .

(b) ATTENDANCE AT MEETINGS

The membership of friendly societies today, judged in terms of attendance at meetings, in lack of interest in the election of officials, in lack of desire for contact with other members of the society, is very largely a passive one and, while there have, no doubt, always been a number of purely passive members of friendly societies, expression of feeling and opinion among older members suggests that in the earlier days of the societies, there were proportionately far more people actively interested in the movement than at present. It is rare today to find a friendly society which has much more than the nucleus of an active membership, or attracts to itself anything like the group loyalty which has in the past characterized such organizations.

One indication of a more active type of membership is attendance at meetings. Of the one hundred and fifty friendly society members with whom we came into contact, only three people said that they attended any sort of meeting (branch or general meeting) *regularly*; not more than twenty-five attended any sort of meeting *occasionally*; the remainder never attended meetings, and merely paid their subscriptions. Branch secretaries invariably stressed the present irregularity of attendance at meetings; and even where there was an increasing branch membership, the increase was not reflected in meeting attendances. The secretary of a friendly society in a northern town, for example, stated that in spite of an increasing membership, at an annual meeting where provision would be made for four hundred members, twenty might come. The secretary of a London branch of one of the affiliated orders, a group with a fairly steady membership, at present one hundred and fifty adults and fourteen juniors, expected about thirty to attend the annual meetings and about ten or twelve at fortnightly meetings. In the latter case the 'ten or twelve' includes committee members.

With some friendly societies, meetings have ceased altogether for lack of support; with others, committee meetings and ordinary pay-in meetings are still fairly well attended, but increasingly fewer members are attending annual meetings or monthly meetings of a more general character.

[(c) SAME INDIFFERENCE OVER ELECTION OF OFFICERS]

(d) ACQUAINTANCE WITH OTHER MEMBERS

Friendly society members were asked whether they knew or wished to know any of the other members of their particular society. Almost invariably, the answer to both questions was 'No' . . .

Acquaintance was restricted to the family, a few neighbours, or a small group of workmates, and there was no particular indication that membership of the same society was regarded as any bond between them. Some older members, and even occasionally younger members, who before the war had taken a more active part in their society, spoke of their enjoyment of the social occasions on which it has been possible to meet other members, but this was not a usual attitude . . .

(e) THE AGE FACTOR

The majority of friendly society members stated that they did not attend meetings; felt no desire to take part in the election of officials; knew very few members of their society and had no wish to meet others. In other words, the attitude of the individual member towards active participation in friendly society organization is negative and resistant.

So far as the immediate future of the friendly societies is concerned these results are not encouraging. They are less so, the more obvious it becomes that, on the whole, these negative attitudes are more pronounced among younger people, and that friendly society membership today tends towards the older age-groups. Most friendly society secretaries stressed the fact that younger members were not now joining the societies to the extent necessary to balance the older membership, most of them believing that younger people were less interested in saving at the present time than they had ever been.

D2 Mass Observation's Study of One Society (pp. 24–6)

This friendly society is one which in terms of membership, activities and enthusiasm, in everything but in exacting goodwill and financial security, is in process of decay; a group which looks backwards over a period of fifty years when it was a live social organism, and forward, with faint hope, to an uncertain future.

Three-quarters of its members are over forty-five years of age. Twenty years ago there were 120 members; today there are 85. No one is quite sure how many came to general meetings in the early days of the society, but it is believed that nearly all the members did so. In 1930, forty people would come: immediately before the war, a dozen; today, none. During the war, the hall previously hired for meetings remained unblacked-out, and so unused. No effort is now being made to hold general meetings, because, says the secretary:

Although, according to the rules, we should have meetings on the first and third Wednesdays of every month . . . all the members know that they can come to my house if they want to hold a meeting. A lot of them have moved away from the district, and they send their contributions by post; I only see them when they want anything or when they are sick.

The society has, naturally, a management committee: seven people who constitute the only people taking an active part in affairs. Even these, it seems, are not *very* active, and, in fact, the secretary and the treasurer do most of the work. No ordinary member now has any say in the election of officers. Again, 'according to the rules', officers should come up for election at the annual general meeting. But as no general meetings have taken place since the war, members of the Management Committee remain officials as long as they wish; if one dies, another, 'one of the older members', says the secretary, is co-opted in his place.

In the early days of the group, there were all kinds of social events, and some of the older members look back regretfully to the heyday of the society . . .

If the financial inducement is the only one offered by the friendly society, and a National Insurance Scheme offers wide benefits at a *compulsorily* increased rate, what are the chances that younger people will join and revive the movement? It does seem that something more than the additional insurance benefit will be required, and certainly something more than a mere *wish* for new and younger members, such as is felt by the secretary of this particular group, who told us that:

We lost a lot of members through the war. Of course, we always *hope* for new members. The head office has put forward different schemes for increasing membership but I'm not very clear about them. Twenty years ago we ran a series of dances to try and attract new members, but although we didn't lose any money on them, we didn't get any new members.

And even if someone did respond to this *hope*, he would not, it seems, be made to feel that he was joining a group which had any but financial benefits to offer him, for:

We don't have initiation ceremonies any more. We just get a doctor's certificate for them, and I inform the committee, and that's that!

Conclusion:
a Verdict on Beveridge's
Collectivism

Like much else in Britain in recent years, our understanding of
Beveridge is being pushed backwards and to the right. This point can
be illustrated by considering the account of Beveridge which Correlli
Barnett presents in his book *The Audit of War* (1986). The substance
of Barnett's account is not new for he accepts the received opinion
that the Beveridge of the 1940s was an ambitious left collectivist who
wished to extend the sphere of state action. But if we compare
Barnett's account with that of Harris (1977), then it is clear that the
tone has changed quite fundamentally; if Harris represents historio-
graphy then Barnett represents demonology. Beveridge's collectivism is in this process and climate being not so much observed as
roundly abused. Barnett argues vigorously that Beveridge in the
1940s represented a kind of Utopian leftism about 'New Jerusalem'
which was disastrous in the long run because its legacy was a policy
settlement which worsened the British disease. The textual evidence
for Barnett's view is very limited. We have used extensive extracts
and our editorial commentaries to establish a very different view of
Beveridge. If Beveridge's policy strategy of the 1940s was Utopian,
that was because Beveridge made so many concessions to the individ-
ualistic premisses of liberal capitalism which he still accepted.
Furthermore, although the policy settlement of the late 1940s was an
important influence on the world in which we now live, in our view
Beveridge, as architect of this settlement, should not as a result be
held responsible for the economic decline of postwar Britain. This
conclusion aims to draw together our arguments about these issues.
Before we turn to this task, it is useful to summarize and criticize
Barnett's position on Beveridge's collectivism.

On Barnett's account, real economic problems and priorities were
neglected by an '"enlightened" establishment which strove in

wartime for the vision of a New Jerusalem' (Barnett, 1986, p. 26). This establishment had a social vision of a postwar Britain where there would be fair shares for all, comprehensive social security, free medicine and full employment. The enlightened establishment included 'prophets' such as Archbishop Temple, the Labour front bench, socialist intellectuals like Laski, the Commonwealth party and Beveridge who was 'the most important single influence on public opinion with regard to the postwar era, New Jerusalem incarnate' (Barnett, 1986, p. 45). On this account the 1942 report on social insurance and the 1944 report on full employment figure as the common prayer books of the new creed. The 1942 text is rubbished by reiterating the criticisms of Beveridge's opponents in the government apparatus, especially in the Treasury. These argued that post-war Britain could not afford comprehensive social security; the unlikely hero of Barnett's account is the wartime Chancellor Kingsley Wood who in a note about the 1942 report asked, 'Is this the time to assume that the general taxpayer has a bottomless purse?' (Barnett, 1986, p. 47). The Keynesianism of the 1944 report is presented as equally unrealistic; it never confronts the problems such as cost push inflation which would arise in a full employment economy and ignores the real economic issue of whether an impoverished and second-rate national economy like Britain could compete successfully in a new international economy after 1945.

If New Jerusalem promoted irrelevant and pernicious policies, Barnett believes that was because its prophets were primarily concerned with ethical ends rather than technical instruments:

> New Jerusalem was simply a matter of applying the Ten Commandments to a twentieth-century industrial society and choosing . . . the most morally righteous system. (Barnett, 1986, p. 44)

Ultimately, Beveridge is guilty by virtue of the moral tone which he shares with Archbishop Temple and Harold Laski. The 1942 report is offensive because as a contemporary critic observed 'the Beveridge report conveys insidiously the suggestion that a good time can be had by all, the moment the last shot is fired' (Harris, 1977, p. 423). Not so, according to Barnett, who believes that the attempt to construct a brave new world after 1945 not only ignored but also aggravated the problems of the cruel real world. The British economy in the Second World War already 'manifested the classic symptoms of what was later to be dubbed "the British disease"' (Barnett, 1986, p. 51). And the long-run consequences of the post-1945 policy settlement were disastrous, for

> in the long term the welfare state would become, just as Kingsley Wood forewarned, a prior charge on the national income of ever more monstrous size, and finally [accounting for] 40 per cent of public expenditure, uncontrollably guzzling taxes which might have gone into productive investment and spewing them out again indiscriminately to the poor and prosperous. (Barnett, 1986, p. 241)

If there is much to criticize in Barnett's account of Beveridge, that is because his whole interpretation rests on the questionable assumptions that the postwar policy settlement played a major role in our subsequent economic decline and that there was a realistic alternative economic strategy which would have directed resources into industry. Barnett's argument on these issues is unsatisfactory because his book cuts between and simply juxtaposes a stereotype of New Jerusalem and journalistic images and assertions about the nature and causes of our economic decline in the 1980s. Barnett does not therefore recognize the way in which the principles of economic policy changed when Labour lost office in 1951. The postwar Labour government presided over an austere system where exports, capital investment and all kinds of government expenditure including defence expenditure were increased so that consumers obtained a relatively small proportion of the increase in national income (Pollard, 1962, pp. 375–6; Cairncross, 1985). After the Korean war, the Tories were able to run down defence expenditure and engineer a private consumption boom in a full employment economy which was growing at 2 per cent per annum.

In both phases of policy, before and after 1951, there is no evidence that government policy diverted funds from private, productive, economic uses to public, unproductive, social uses. As Matthews (1968) showed long ago, this kind of 'crowding out' argument is implausible because private investment expenditure was maintained at a high level throughout the long postwar boom. Furthermore, it is not clear that increasing the volume of private investment would have improved manufacturing performance if, as Barnett admits, there were management and labour problems in British industry. If there never was an alternative strategy of the

Barnett kind, we also doubt whether the prevailing economic and social policies have played an important role in Britain's decline after 1951. This decline has been motored by the uncompetitiveness of British manufacturing which since the early 1970s has failed to increase output and maintain value added and employment. We have examined the causes of this failure elsewhere (Williams *et al.*, 1983) and argued that government policy played a secondary, passive role. Much more important at the institutional level was the way in which enterprise calculation was constrained by private financial institutions like the banks and the stock exchange. Quite apart from the adverse conditioning, enterprise calculation was itself deficient because time horizons were short and British management was generally inept at organizing production and marketing (Cutler *et al.*, 1986). There is no discernible connection between these failings and the economic and social policies which Beveridge advocated.

If we are concerned to characterize those policies, it is hard to recognize the Beveridge of this reader in Barnett's account because Barnett never analyses any of Beveridge's texts at length and he is often factually incorrect about the nature of Beveridge's positions on particular issues. For example, it is simply not true that Beveridge neglected the issue of the cost of his social insurance scheme. As our extracts in Chapter 2 show, Beveridge in 1942 insisted that the scheme was financially practical and showed that it required a modest redistribution of resources on a scale which would have been possible before 1939; as he later observed, 'to assume that we must be indefinitely poorer after the war than before it is reasonless defeatism' (*Pillars of Security*, 1943, p. 123). The social insurance scheme was deliberately and explicitly set up by Beveridge so that a large part of the cost was covered by employee contributions which were transfer payments within the working class. General taxation (via the Treasury contribution) and employers (via the employer contribution) only topped up the fund; as Kincaid (1973) has argued, in most European countries after 1945 employers paid a much larger proportion of the cost of social insurance. Moreover, at the time Britain was, Switzerland and Sweden aside, the wealthiest country in Europe.

It could be argued that the expenditure burden of social insurance should not be considered in isolation; Barnett clearly believes that the cost of insurance and assistance, plus family allowances, plus a health service, was more than 'the economy could afford' (Barnett,

1986, p. 45). But that point is not self-evidently true. Beveridge recognized that in the short run there would be problems about 'when we can afford the whole Security Plan' (*Pillars of Security*, 1943, p. 123); devices like the proposed 20-year lead into the payment of full old age pensions were designed to deal with this problem. But in the long run cost was not a problem because Beveridge put his faith in what the next generation would call economic growth; 'there will be ample in total after this war if we can use our productive resources in productive employment' (*Pillars of Security*, 1943, p. 76).

On some points Barnett more or less inverts Beveridge's position. For example, it is alleged that New Jerusalem privileged social policy objectives at the expense of economic policy objectives. On the contrary, as our extracts show, Beveridge realized that all of Britain's human and capital resources would have to work efficiently and productively if his social plans were to succeed; that was why he went on to write his second report on full employment. Barnett (1986, p. 47) charges that in this report, and elsewhere, Beveridge was unreasonably preoccupied with grand objectives and glossed over the issues of how these objectives were to be achieved. There is no doubt that some policy documents of the 1940s were guilty of this offence; the 1944 official White Paper on full employment never specified the means by which this end could be achieved. But it is bizarre to accuse Beveridge of such an offence when so much space and effort in the 1942 and 1944 reports was devoted to specifying the technical instruments of social insurance and demand management which were designed for the tasks of abolishing poverty and maintaining full employment. Beveridge's popular success in the 1940s rested on the general belief that his new technical instruments could deliver these objectives (and do so without undermining the liberal capitalist order). There is a serious question about why these policy instruments increasingly failed to deliver the objectives; but that question cannot be posed or answered inside the circle of misrepresentations which constitutes Barnett's account of Beveridge.

On our alternative account, the failure of the policies which Beveridge advocated to curb unemployment and eliminate poverty was inevitable because Beveridge's commitment to individualism and preserving the freedoms of capitalism undermined the possibility of effective action. We agree that Beveridge was a Utopian but where Barnett would blame the unreal ambition of Beveridge's leftism, we would blame the real persistence of rightist elements in Beveridge's liberal collectivism. This point emerges clearly if we consider Beveridge's economic or social policies and we can begin by considering the failure of Keynesian demand management.

Since the early 1970s there has been increasing criticism of Keynesian theory as a way of understanding the world. In their different ways both monetarists and rational expectations theorists claim to have revolutionized the macro-economics which Keynes created; the expectations theorists, for example, flatly deny the *General Theory*'s central proposition that irrational business expectations determine the volume of private investment. For our immediate purposes, it is not necessary to judge these claims. The point we would make is the more modest one that Keynesianism, or the technique of demand management, could not function as a way of changing the world because its conditions of application are seldom satisfied, and they certainly were not satisfied in Britain after the Second World War. Interestingly enough, this line of criticism is similar to Keynes's own criticism of neo-classical economics and its policy of wage reductions as a cure for unemployment. As we have argued elsewhere (Cutler *et al.*, 1986), in the *General Theory* Keynes responded with the argument that such policies might work in principle but in practice they were irrelevant because they required a preliminary attack on trade unions and free collective bargaining which was not politically feasible or desirable.

If the neo-classical wage-cutting cure for unemployment requires conditions of application which cannot be satisfied, much the same point can be made about the Keynesian reflationary cure for unemployment. This treatment cannot be applied because it requires economic and political preconditions which are seldom satisfied; the national economy where Keynesianism is applied, must have a healthy balance of payments surplus and co-operative or compliant financial institutions. Economically, substantial unilateral reflation is usually impossible for a single open economy with a precarious trade balance. In such circumstances, the resulting expansion of demand will draw in imports so that a balance of payments crisis ensues. Under the rules of sound finance, a payments crisis requires deflation and a deficit-running country is in no position to resist the terms set by private lenders or public institutions like the IMF. Until North Sea oil came on stream in the later 1970s, the British balance of payments was always precarious and there were recurrent payments crises every five or six years. And in the late 1980s, a much worse payments crisis looms when the price of oil has been halved and the oil is beginning to run out; the uncompetitiveness of British manufacturing is such that we now have a large and growing deficit in manufacturing which oil increasingly will not cover. If the economic preconditions make Keynesianism problematic and irrelevant to Britain's predicament, there are also political difficulties because reflation requires deficit financing which in Western countries usually requires the sale of government bonds to private financial institutions which are not obliged to buy government paper if they have no confidence in government policies. Financial institutions can always obstruct Keynesian reflation through what in Britain we would call a 'gilts strike'.

The argument so far is instructive because it helps to explain the central paradox of postwar economic policy; Keynesian demand management was used throughout the 1950s and 1960s for 'fine-tuning' a full employment economy but it was never tried in the 1970s and 1980s when unemployment was high and rising. In the first period Keynesianism was the Treasury's toy but it could not be used in a more serious way when it was really needed because its economic and political conditions of application were not satisfied. The moral is that this kind of centrism must be rejected as Utopian and it is necessary to make a political choice between the right and left solutions to unemployment. The choice is political because (as Keynes argued) the wage reduction solution can only be made to work if the freedoms of the unionized working class are abridged and because (as we would argue) the reflationary solution can only be made to work if the freedoms of capitalist enterprises and their owners are abridged. Either way it is necessary to contemplate an abridgement of freedom which Beveridge hoped to avoid. If the British left now wishes to tackle unemployment through reflation, it must curb the freedom of firms, financial institutions and individuals to do what they will with their own. Some form of restraint on imports is necessary if injected purchasing power is not to leak abroad and create a payments crisis; that means limiting the consumer's choice of imported manufactures. Furthermore, government deficits can only be financed if financial institutions are encouraged or compelled to hold government paper in the required quantity; that means restricting the freedom of financial institutions to arrange their asset portfolios. Regulation and/or social ownership would also presumably have to be used for the manufacturing firms who now have the freedom to invest and divest.

In the sphere of the social, Beveridge's liberal collectivist promise of the best of both worlds is equally Utopian for reasons which we have analysed in the introductions to the relevant chapters of this reader. Poverty cannot be abolished by social insurance because the politically congenial technique of social insurance cannot be extended to cover the whole field of income maintenance. It was certain that a Beveridge-style flat rate insurance scheme could not do the job because, as long as flat rate contributions were levied, the insurance fund would never have a substantial and elastic revenue base from which dependence could be supported. Furthermore, the morally congenial institutions of voluntary action did not have the vitality to win out against selfishness and the business motive; the field of private welfare after 1945 was dominated by occupational pension funds rather than friendly societies. It could be argued that the institutions of voluntary action might have won out if, as Beveridge intended, the state had supported them with a suitable regime of tax concessions. But the results of such a regime would almost certainly have disappointed Beveridge who favoured the institutions of voluntary action in so far as they represented the values of mutual aid and philanthropy. The building societies which did obtain tax concessions only became the Frankenstein monsters of private welfare. They diverted funds into an inflation of exchange values rather than encouraging new house construction and they created a huge vested interest in mortgage tax relief which was the most regressive of tax subsidies. This result suggests that a more complete implementation of the Beveridge strategy would only have worsened our present predicament.

As it was, if Beveridge promised the best of both worlds, in social welfare terms he helped create the worst of all possible worlds which combined an ineffectual state system of basic income maintenance and an overdeveloped private system of occupational welfare. After 1945, in the vacant space above the state minimum, selfish forms of private saving expanded to fill the area which in Beveridge's fantasy was to be occupied by altruisic mutuality. Occupational welfare (pensions, company cars, BUPA, etc.) refreshed the parts which voluntary action did not reach. The development of occupational welfare created the most serious problem of all because it was tax-subvented. The middle classes and their subalterns increasingly lived in a world of tax-relieved mortgages, tax-exempt pensions and undertaxed company cars. This development created a new vested interest in the status quo which is as unacceptable to the radical right as to the egalitarian left. That vested interest now powerfully obstructs any radical social reform by the left or right; the 1980s Tory government and its Labour opposition were both afraid to claim the revenue which is forgone through the panoply of tax concessions. Unless some of this lost revenue is claimed and used to supplement graduated insurance contributions or direct taxation, it is hard to see how the deficiencies of the income maintenance system can be rectified.

And this conclusion helps us towards a verdict on Beveridge's social collectivism. Beveridge did put social security on the wrong principles. We should forgive him that because, after all, in the long run we are all wrong just as surely as we are all dead. In abstract terms it is always possible to reconceptualize the problem of income maintenance, redefine the techniques and propose that social security be put on different principles. But the implementation of such proposals may be practically difficult or impossible if vested private interests obstruct reform. The creation of a massive vested interest in the status quo was the unintended social legacy of Beveridge's liberal collectivism.

Liberal collectivism of the 1940s was an intellectually ingenious reconciliation of opposed values and its early achievements may have been substantial. But this recently invented political ideology is now nearing its end because our current problems are not amenable to liberal collectivist treatment and indeed have been partly created by liberal collectivism. Again and again our argument has brought us to the problem which Beveridge in the 1940s could not confront; either state intervention against poverty and insecurity is much less effective than Beveridge wanted it to be or state intervention must be pushed further until it threatens at least some of the capitalist political and economic freedoms which Beveridge wished to protect. If, like Beveridge, we are not prepared to accept the world as it is, then we must now make that direct choice between capitalism and socialism from which Beveridge in the 1940s tried to escape.

William (later Lord) Beveridge:
An Outline Life

William Beveridge was born in Rangpur, Bengal on 5 March 1879, and died on 16 March 1963 at his Oxford home.

He was the second child and eldest son of Henry Beveridge, a district session judge in the Indian Civil Service.

He was educated at Charterhouse and Balliol where he gained firsts in Classical and Mathematical Moderations and then in Greats (1901). He took the degree of BCL in 1903 and from 1902–9 was Stowell Civil Law Fellow of University College, Oxford.

From 1903–5 he was sub-warden of Toynbee Hall, the Oxford University settlement in the East End of London, and investigated unemployment in the London docks.

In 1905 he was a member of the semi-official Central Unemployed Body set up under the Unemployed Workmen Act of that year. He became chairman of its committee which promoted the first London labour exchanges.

From 1906–8 he was a prolific leader-writer for the Conservative *Morning Post*. In 1908 he entered Whitehall initially as a non-established civil servant acting as personal assistant to Winston Churchill, recently appointed as President of the Board of Trade in the Liberal administration.

In the Board of Trade Beveridge with Llewellyn Smith as his head of department worked to create the first national system of labour exchanges under an Act of 1909 and, under the Act of 1911, set up a compulsory unemployment insurance scheme.

In 1915 he went to the Ministry of Munitions and in 1916 to the Ministry of Food from whence he launched the first national rationing scheme during the last year of the First World War.

He became permanent secretary at the ministry in 1919 but left in the same year, persuaded by the Webbs to take up the post of Director of LSE where he stayed till 1937. He did much to transform the LSE from a small institution into a leading university centre of learning.

During his time there he undertook various public duties, serving as a member of the Royal Commission on Coal (Samuel Commission) from 1925–6, as chairman of the Unemployment Insurance Statutory Committee (1933–4), and as Vice-Chancellor of London University (1926–8).

He was Master of University College, Oxford from 1937–44, became Liberal MP for Berwick-on-Tweed at a by-election in October 1944 but was defeated by a Conservative in the general election of 1945.

During the Second World War he conducted a survey of the nation's manpower for Ernest Bevin, and then became chairman of what started as an interdepartmental committee on social insurance and allied services. This body he transformed into an advisory committee serving him as chairman and, as such, he produced the famous 'Beveridge Report' of 1942. The coalition government gave it a cool reception but public opinion was enthusiastic and forced action.

After the war he served as chairman of two development corporations (Aycliffe, 1947, and Peterlee, 1949) and conducted an official inquiry (1949–51) into the future of broadcasting.

In 1942 he married the widow of his cousin David Mair. Janet Mair had been Beveridge's secretary both during the First World War and during his time at the LSE.

In 1916 he was created CB, in 1919 KCB; in 1949 he was made a baron and sat in the House of Lords as a Liberal.

Compiled from *The Times* obituary, and the *DNB* entry written by Jose Harris who has produced the definitive biography, *William Beveridge: a biography* (1977), Oxford, which also contains a list of Beveridge's main writings.

Notes

General Introduction

1   Hobson, John Atkinson (1858–1940). A 'new liberal' economist and writer who devoted his main energies to economic and social studies on which he published thirty-five works as well as numerous pamphlets and articles. He was an independent thinker who directly challenged orthodox economic theories. In particular he formulated a theory of under-consumption first developed with A. F. Mummery in *The Physiology of Industry* (1889) and extended in such works as *The Economics of Distribution* (1900), *Imperialism* (1902) and *The Industrial System* (1909). After 1897 he was never offered a university post though his reputation was partly, and inadequately, redeemed by J. M. (later Lord) Keynes's references in *The General Theory* (1936).
2   Hobhouse, Leonard Trelawney (1864–1929). A liberal philosopher and journalist who surrendered an Oxford fellowship in 1897 to work as a leader-writer for the *Manchester Guardian* and then, in 1907, became first professor of sociology at London University. Of his pre-1914 books the most immediately relevant are *Democracy and Reaction* (1904), *Social Evolution and Political Theory* (1911) and *Development and Purpose* (1913).
3   Macmillan, Harold (later Earl of Stockton) (1894–1987). Politician, publisher and writer. Conservative M.P. for Stockton-on-Tees 1924–9 and 1931–1945, Bromley Div. of Kent 1945–64. Numerous ministerial offices. Prime Minister 1957–63. Of his numerous books *The Middle Way* (1937) represented a major and influential centrist attempt to propose substantial intervention in the private enterprise system so as to avoid more drastic socialist solutions and preserve a capitalistic freedom.

Chapter 1

1   Rowntree, Benjamin Seebohm (1871–1954). A Quaker manufacturer associated with the family firm of Rowntree & Co. from 1889 to 1941. Now remembered as a social investigator who published a number of important works on social conditions. This began with *Poverty, a Study of Town Life* (1901), a survey of York which was carried on in *Poverty and Progress* (1941), the second York survey, and (with G. R. Lavers) *Poverty and the Welfare State* (1951), the third York survey. Amongst

179

other works the most relevant to the present study is *Unemployment, A Social Study* (1911) written with Bruno Lasker, and *How the Labourer Lives* (1913) with May Kendall.
2   See General Introduction, note 1.
3   See General Introduction, note 3.
4   Mises, Ludwig Edler von (1881–1973). The leading twentieth-century figure of the Austrian School of Economics. A major contribution was his argument that rational allocation of resources was not possible under socialist planning which dispensed with a true price system. On this basis he developed a general critique of government intervention. *Socialism: an Economic and Sociological Analysis* (1922).
5   Hayek, Friedrich A. von (1899–   ). A major protagonist in the cause of a free competitive economic system and an important intellectual source of the new radical right epitomized in Mrs Thatcher's governments after 1979. His most influential book is *The Road to Serfdom* (1944).
6   Robbins, Lionel (1898–   ). As Professor of Economics at the LSE from 1929–61, Robbins in the 1930s was a vigorous exponent of orthodox free market economics. An active public figure, he was chairman of the Committee on Higher Education, 1961–4, which produced the Robbins Report, a blueprint for the expansion of the universities.
7   Friendly societies were the means by which small tradesmen and the working class provided against sickness, old age and the expenses of burial. They were insurance societies based on mutual principles. A major social institution in the nineteenth century, they were still of significance up to the Second World War.
8   The establishment of the Milk Marketing Board in 1933 led to protracted disputes between farmers, government and manufacturers about the different prices which should be charged to different categories of users.
9   Wartime regulations issued under the Emergency Powers legislation of 1939 which gave the Minister of Labour powers to control the use of labour. By 1942 some 8 million workers were tied to their jobs by essential work orders.

Chapter 2

1   See Chapter 1, note 1. Rowntree's intensive study *Poverty, a Study of Town Life* (1901) became known as the first York survey after he repeated the investigation and published the results in 1941 and 1951.
2   The Royal Commission on the Poor Laws and Relief of Distress, appointed by the Conservative government in 1905, presented two major reports – Majority and Minority – in 1909. The Minority report urging the abolition of the poor law and the redistribution of its functions was written by Sidney and Beatrice Webb, the famous Fabian partners in the field of social investigation.
3   Charles Booth (1840–1916) was a shipowner and writer on social

questions. He carried out a major social inquiry in the capital which was published in 17 volumes as *Life and Labour of the People of London* (1891–1903).

4 Approved societies were established under the 1911 National Health Insurance Act to administer the cash benefits under the scheme. Originally intended only for friendly societies, approved society status was subsequently conferred on any society which formed a separate section for the purpose. The effect was to extend the title to industrial life offices, trade unions and employers' provident funds.

5 On the basis of the report of the Royal Commission of Unemployment Insurance set up in 1929, a bill authorizing 'anomalies regulations' was passed in July 1931. The regulations were aimed at ending certain abuses in the system and they had the effect of depriving some classes of unemployed persons, mainly married women, of benefit.

Chapter 3

1 In 1934 Beveridge became chairman of the Unemployment Insurance Statutory Committee, one of the many ways in which he continued to engage in public activities during his period as Director of LSE from 1919 to 1937.

2 The Royal Commission on the Poor Laws and Relief of Distress, appointed in 1905, submitted its two reports (Majority and Minority) in 1909; see Chapter 2, note 2.

3 Labour exchanges were first established on a national basis by Winston Churchill under the Liberal goverment's Labour Exchanges Act, 1909. Beveridge intended that their use should be compulsory, i.e. all employers seeking workers and all workers seeking employment should use the labour exchanges.

4 The Third Winter Group published a substantial report of an inquiry undertaken into the conditions of the unemployed during 1922.

5 A report, *Britain's Industrial Future* (1928), was prepared by a Liberal committee of Industrial Inquiry and published in a cheap edition with yellow covers. It had a large circulation and figured in Lloyd George's election campaign in 1929.

6 Report of the Committee on the Economic and Financial Problems of Provision for Old Age (Cmd. 9333 1954).

7 Sir Herbert Llewellyn Smith (1864–1945) was a civil servant and social investigator who first came to public notice through a book (*Story of the Docker' Strike*, 1890) written with Vaughan Nash. He became first commissioner at the newly created Labour Department of the Board of Trade in 1893. He was prominent in the planning of the new system of unemployment insurance in 1911 and had been associated with Beveridge over the establishment of labour exchanges two years earlier.

8 A departmental committee on unemployment insurance was set up under Lord Blanesburgh in 1925 and reported in 1927. It recommended

granting standard benefit to any unemployed person as a statutory right for an indefinite period if he or she could show evidence at each 3-monthly review of having been in insurable employment for 30 weeks in the previous 2 years, and could satisfy a requirement of 'genuinely seeking work'.

9   The Charity Organisation Society was founded in 1869 to tackle the problem of the poor on a systematic basis. The COS allowed only a very minor role to state aid and aimed to distinguish between deserving and undeserving poor by keeping detailed information on individual applicants for relief. They opposed the casual or 'indiscriminate' giving of charity as undermining the independence and self-help they hoped to induce in the poor.

10   The interwar years saw several bouts of intensive 'circulation wars' amongst daily newspapers: amongst the enticements offered in the 1920s was insurance cover for readers; in the 1930s free or cheap editions of the classics were offered.

11   Sir John Anderson (1882–1958), later Lord Waverley, served as Lord President of the Council, 1940–3, and Chancellor of the Exchequer, 1943–5, in the wartime coalition government.

Chapter 4

1   See General Introduction, note 1.
2   Bradlaugh, Charles (1833–91). A free thinker and secularist lecturer and an MP from 1880 to 1891. In 1876 he was tried and sentenced to 6 months' imprisonment and £200 fine (quashed on appeal) for republishing with Annie Besant (1847–1933) a pamphlet on birth control. Annie Besant after a spell of activity with the Fabian Society became interested in theosophy, settled in India and was prominent in the Indian nationalist movement.
3   The solution of sending the 'residuum' of 'unemployables' to farm labour 'colonies' for discipline and possible rehabilitation was one which commanded general attention amongst social investigators in the 1890s and 1900s. The two best-known experiments on these lines were the Salvation Army's colony at Hadleigh in Essex and that at Hollesley Bay set up by the London Central Committee for the Unemployed in 1905.

Chapter 5

1   Departmental Committee on Industrial Assurance and Assurance on the Lives of Children under Ten Years of Age. The committee was chaired by Sir Benjamin Cohen and reported in 1933 (Cmd. 4376).
2   Dividing societies used to exist in great numbers under a variety of names – slate clubs, tontines, Birmingham benefit societies, etc. – and aimed to divide out their funds amongst the members, perhaps on some specified occasion.

3 Holloway and deposit principles related to methods used by some friendly societies in providing for saving as well as mutual assurance. Deposit societies, an institution invented by the Rev. Samuel Best, combined friendly society features (mutual assurance) with savings banks characteristics. Contributions surplus to meeting the member's mutual obligations would accumulate, at interest, to his individual account. The Holloway principle (attributed to H. Holloway, MP) involved an individual member accumulating contributions at interest which were then, at the time needed, converted into an immediate annuity to provide for old age. This gave more flexibility than was possible if, from the outset, the contributions were used to buy a deferred annuity.

4 Affiliated orders were friendly societies which combined a number of lodges (or branches) into a common organization to maintain principles of 'good neighbourliness' while providing sound general and business principles. The best-known were the Manchester Unity of Oddfellows, and the Foresters.

Bibliography

Barnett, C. (1986), *The Audit of War: The Illusion and Reality of Britain as a Great Nation* (London: Macmillan).

Beveridge, W. (1909), *Unemployment: a problem of industry* (London: Longmans, Green, & Co.). Revised edn, 1930 (London: Longmans).

Beveridge, W. (1924), 'Insurance for all and everything', pamphlet, *Daily News Ltd.*, New Way series no. 7.

Beveridge, W. (1936), *The Past and Present of Unemployment Insurance*, Sidney Ball lecture, 7 February 1930.

Beveridge, W. (1942), *Social Insurance and the Allied Services* (London: HMSO).

Beveridge, W. (1943), *Pillars of Security and Other Wartime Essays and Addresses* (London: Allen & Unwin).

Beveridge, W. (1944), *Full Employment in a Free Society* (London: Allen & Unwin).

Beveridge, W. (1944), 'Beveridge on Beveridge', pamphlet (London: Social Security League).

Beveridge, W. (1945), *Why I am a Liberal* (London: Herbert Jenkins).

Beveridge, W. (1948), *Voluntary Action* (London: Allen & Unwin).

Beveridge, W., and Wells, A. (eds) (1948), *The Evidence for Voluntary Action* (London: Allen & Unwin).

Cairncross, A. (1985), *Years of Recovery, British Economic Policy, 1945–51* (London: Macmillan).

Cutler, T., Williams, K., and Williams J. (1986), *Keynes, Beveridge and Beyond* (London: Routledge & Kegan Paul).

Distel, B., and Jakusch, R. (1978), *Concentration Camp, Dachau (Brussels: Comité International de Dachau).*

Durbin, E. (1940), *The Politics of Democratic Socialism* (London: Routledge & Kegan Paul).

Durbin, E. (1949), *Problems of Economic Planning* (London: Routledge & Kegan Paul).

Freeden, M. (1978), *The New Liberalism: An Ideology of Social Reform* (Oxford: Clarendon Press).

George, V. (1968), *Social Security: Beveridge and After* (London: Routledge & Kegan Paul).

Harris, J. (1977), *William Beveridge, A Biography* (Oxford: Clarendon Press).

Jones, G. S. (1971), *Outcast London* (Oxford: Clarendon Press).

Keynes, J. M. (1936), *The General Theory of Employment, Interest and Money* (London: Macmillan).

Bibliography

Keynes, J. M. (1940), *How to Pay for the War* (London: Macmillan).

Kincaid, J. C. (1973), *Poverty and Equality in Britain* (Harmondsworth: Penguin).

Macmillan, H. (1937), *The Middle Way* (London: Macmillan).

Matthews, R. C. O. (1968), 'Why has Britain had full employment since the war?', *Economic Journal*, vol. 77 (Sept), pp. 555–69.

Middleton, R. (1985), *Who's to Benefit?* (London: Verso).

Pollard, S. (1962), *The Development of the British Economy, 1914–50* (London: Arnold).

Tomlinson, J. (1981), *Problems of Economic Policy, 1870–1945* (London: Methuen).

Williams, K. (1981), *From Pauperism to Poverty* (London: Routledge & Kegan Paul).

Williams, K., Williams, J. and Thomas D. (1983), *Why are the British Bad at Manufacturing?* (London: Routledge & Kegan Paul).

Winch, D. (1969), *Economics and Policy* (London: Hodder & Stoughton).

Index

Index

Printed in the United States
by Baker & Taylor Publisher Services

Printed in the United States
by Baker & Taylor Publisher Services